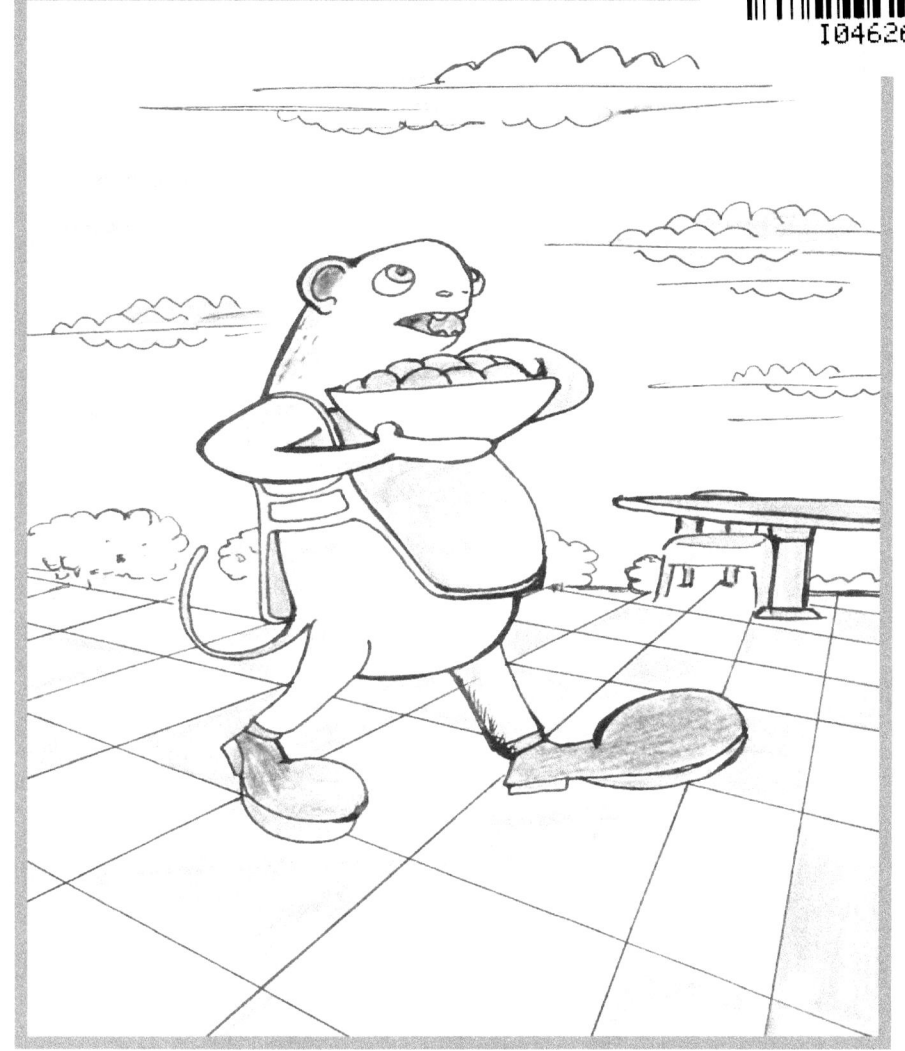

AFRICAN LIFE THEMED
# COLORING BOOK
## catchy arts

50 pictures to color
### WWW.CATCHYARTS.COM
All rights Reserved.

**ISBN: 9781082781353**

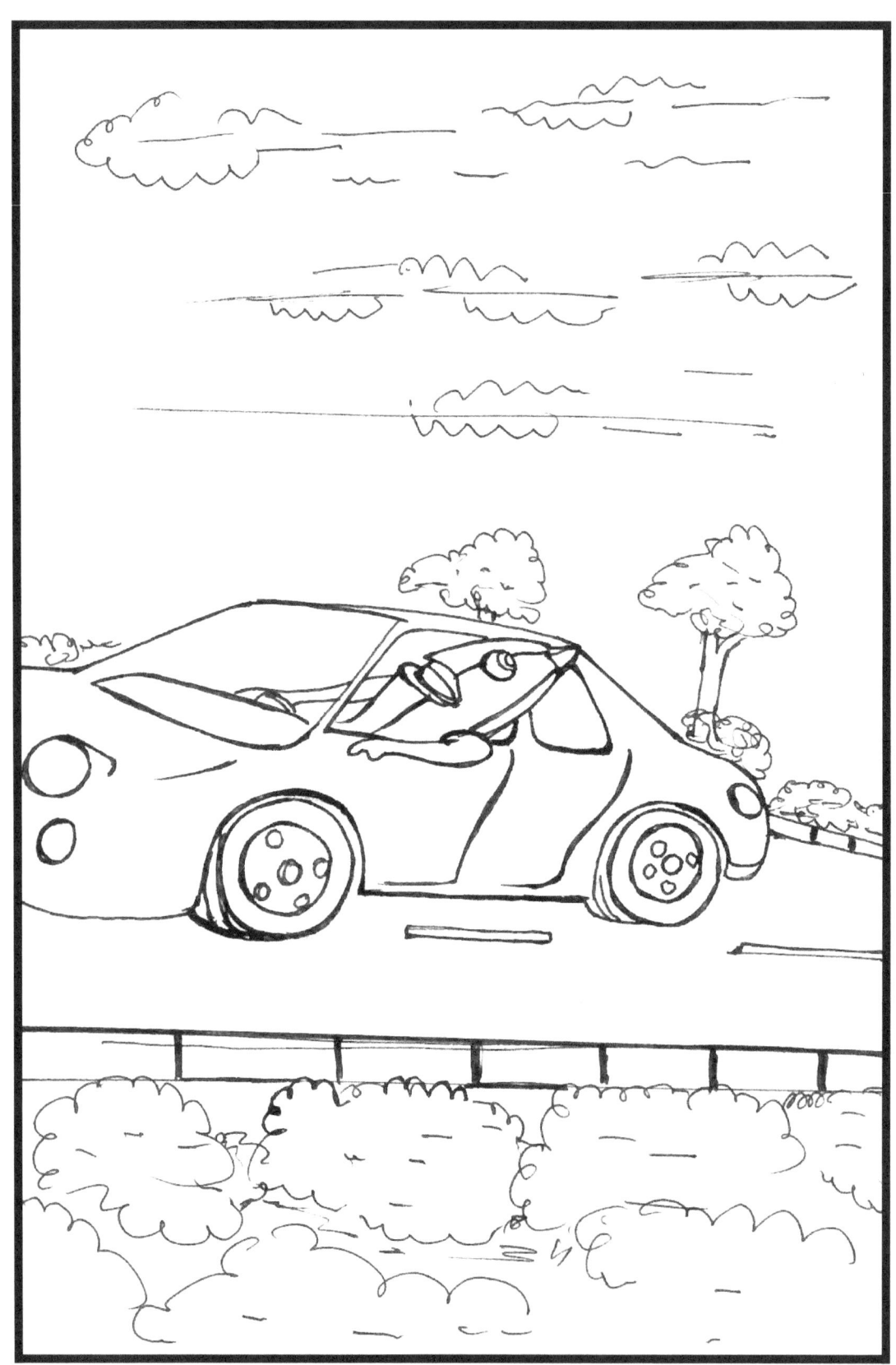

Mr. Pencil driving a car

AFRICAN LIFE THEMED
# COLORING BOOK
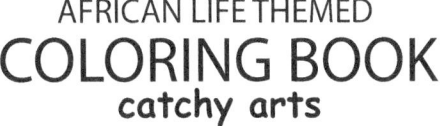
catchy arts

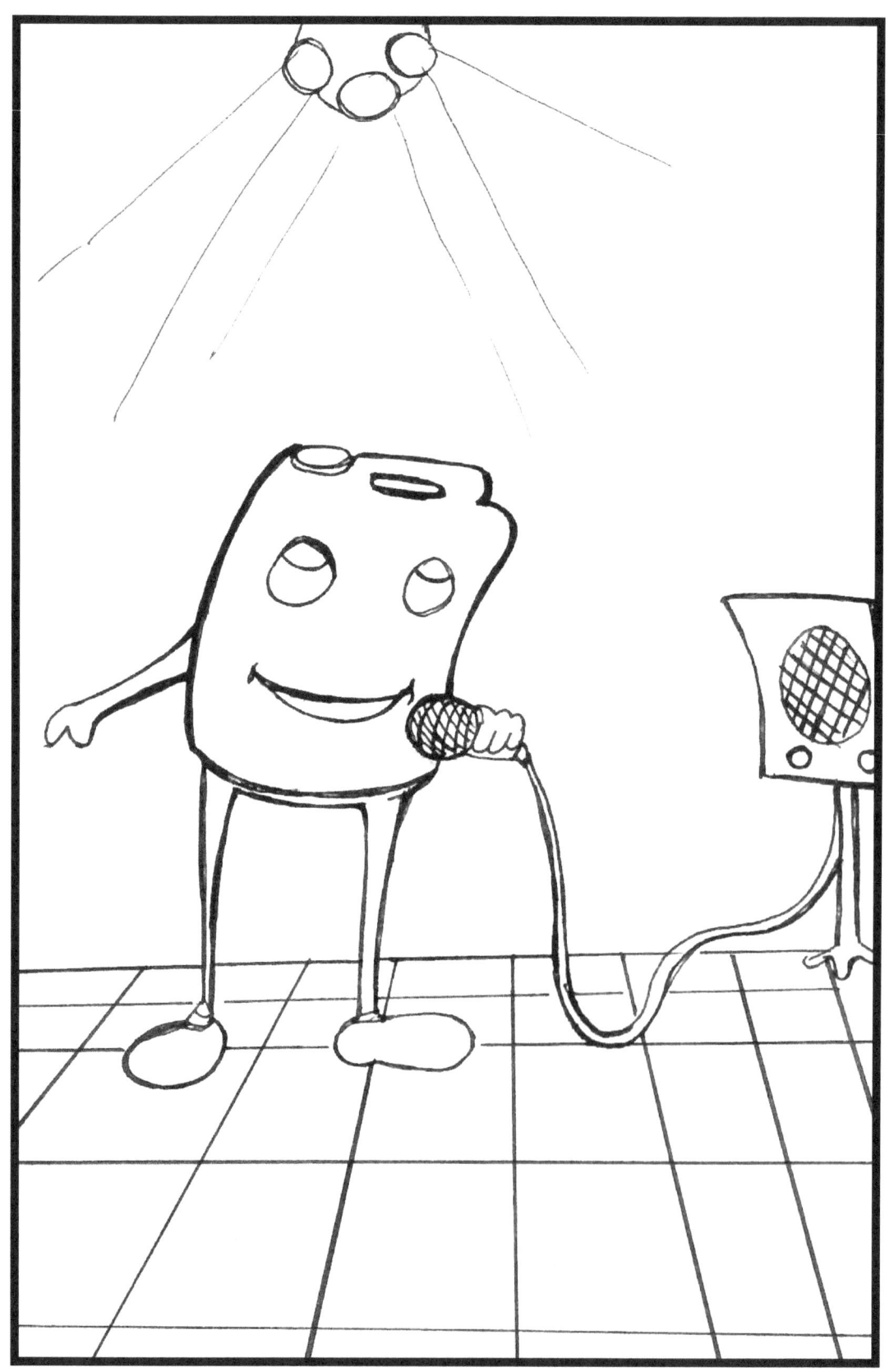

Miss Jerrycan singing while dancing

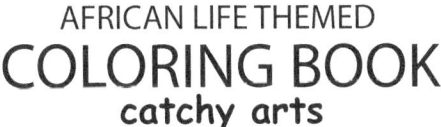

AFRICAN LIFE THEMED
# COLORING BOOK
catchy arts

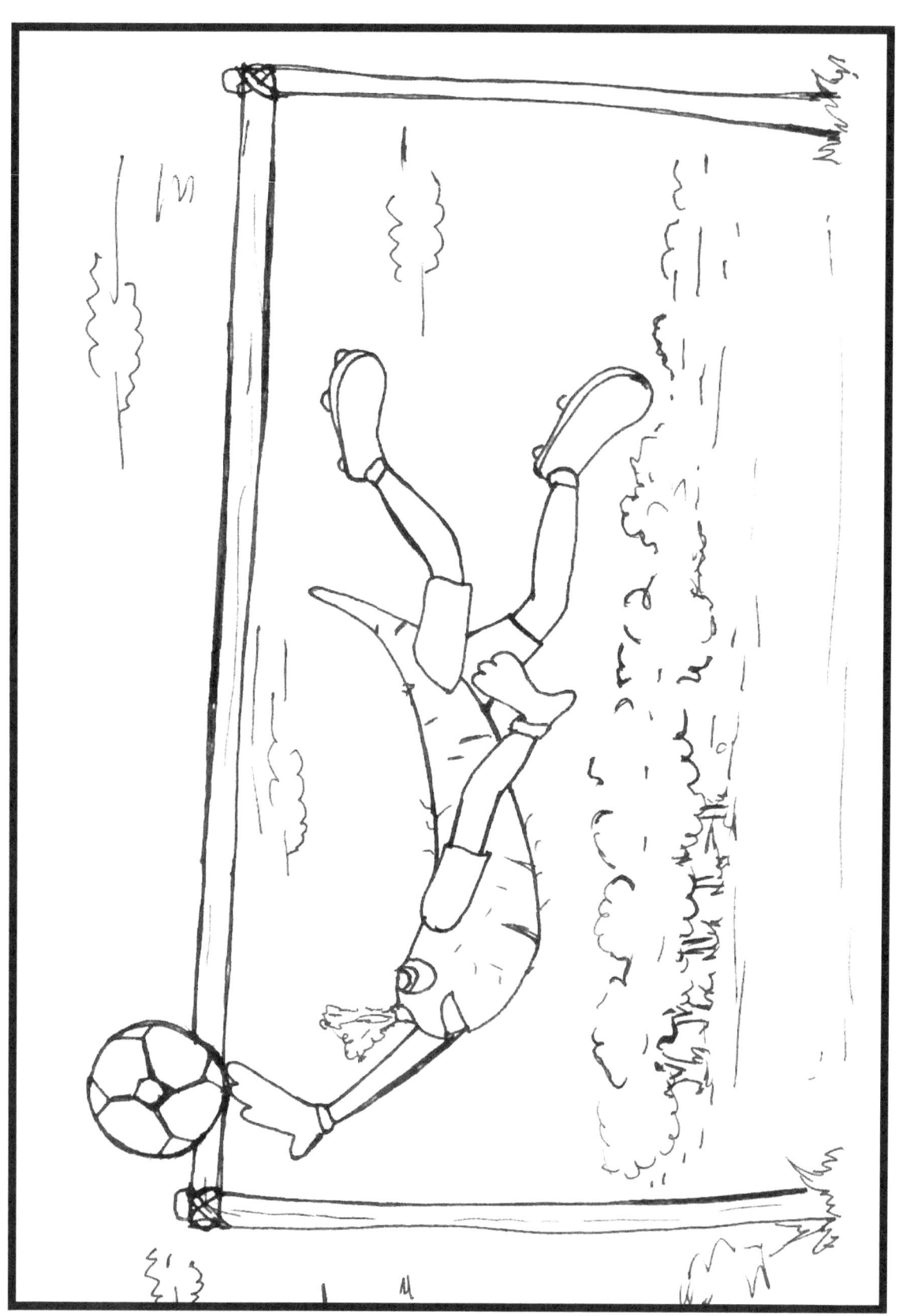

Peter the grasshoper is catching a soccer ball.

AFRICAN LIFE THEMED
# COLORING BOOK
catchy arts

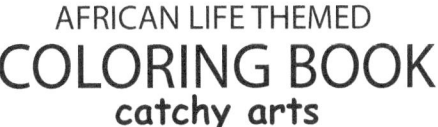

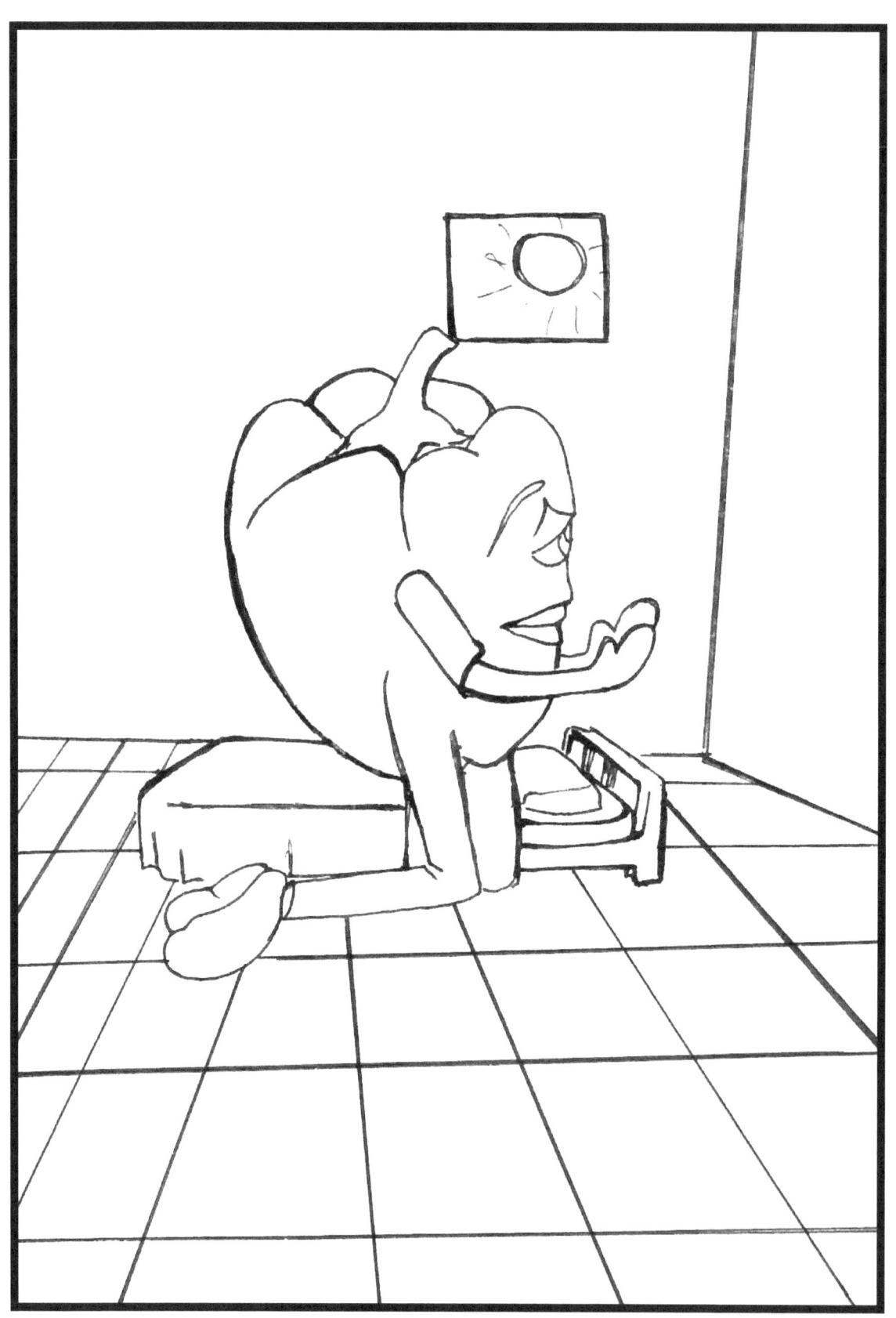

David the pumpkin is praying to God

AFRICAN LIFE THEMED
# COLORING BOOK
catchy arts

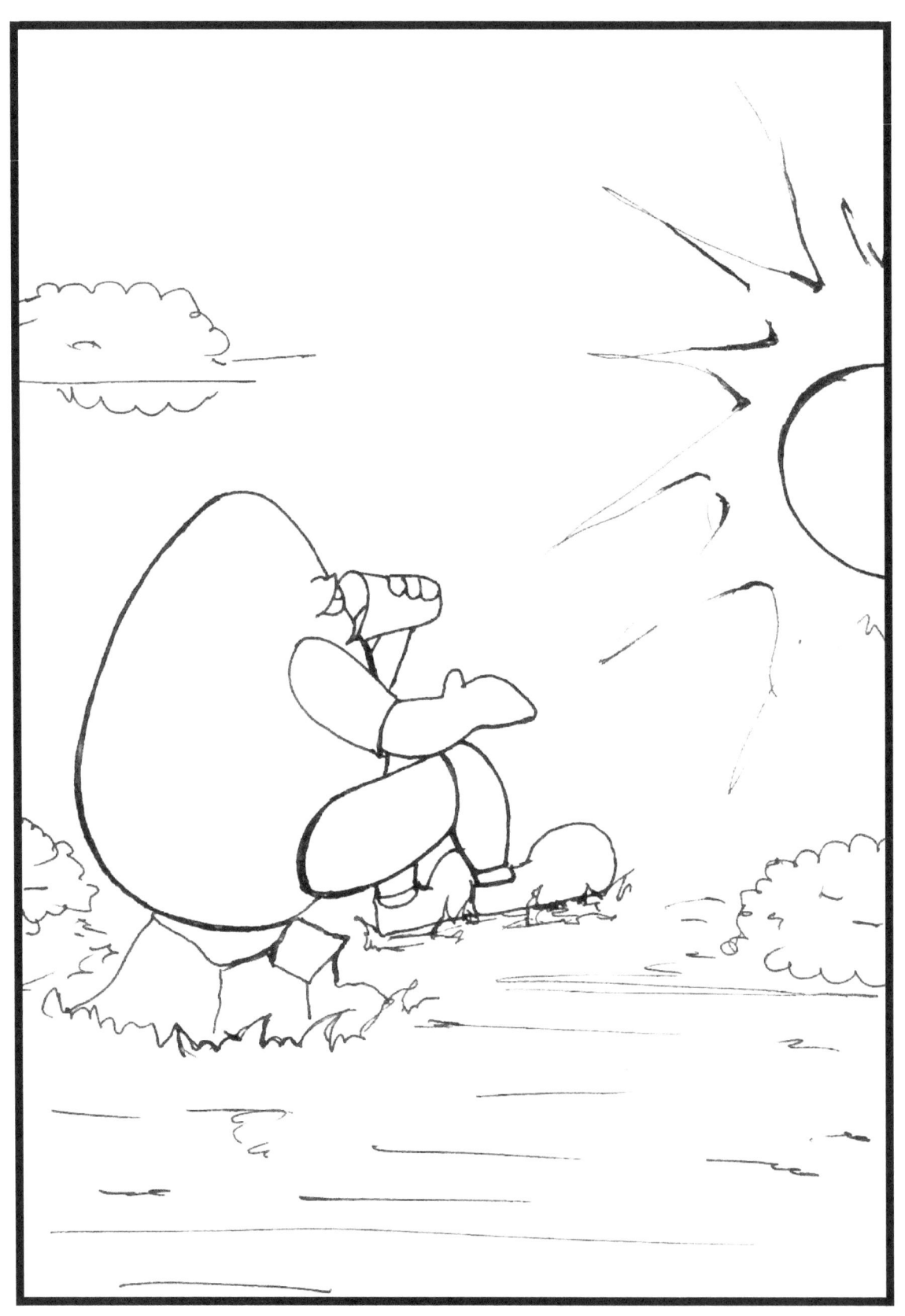

Ann the egg is drinking water while bathing the sun

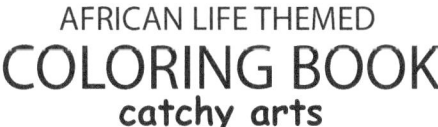

AFRICAN LIFE THEMED
# COLORING BOOK
catchy arts

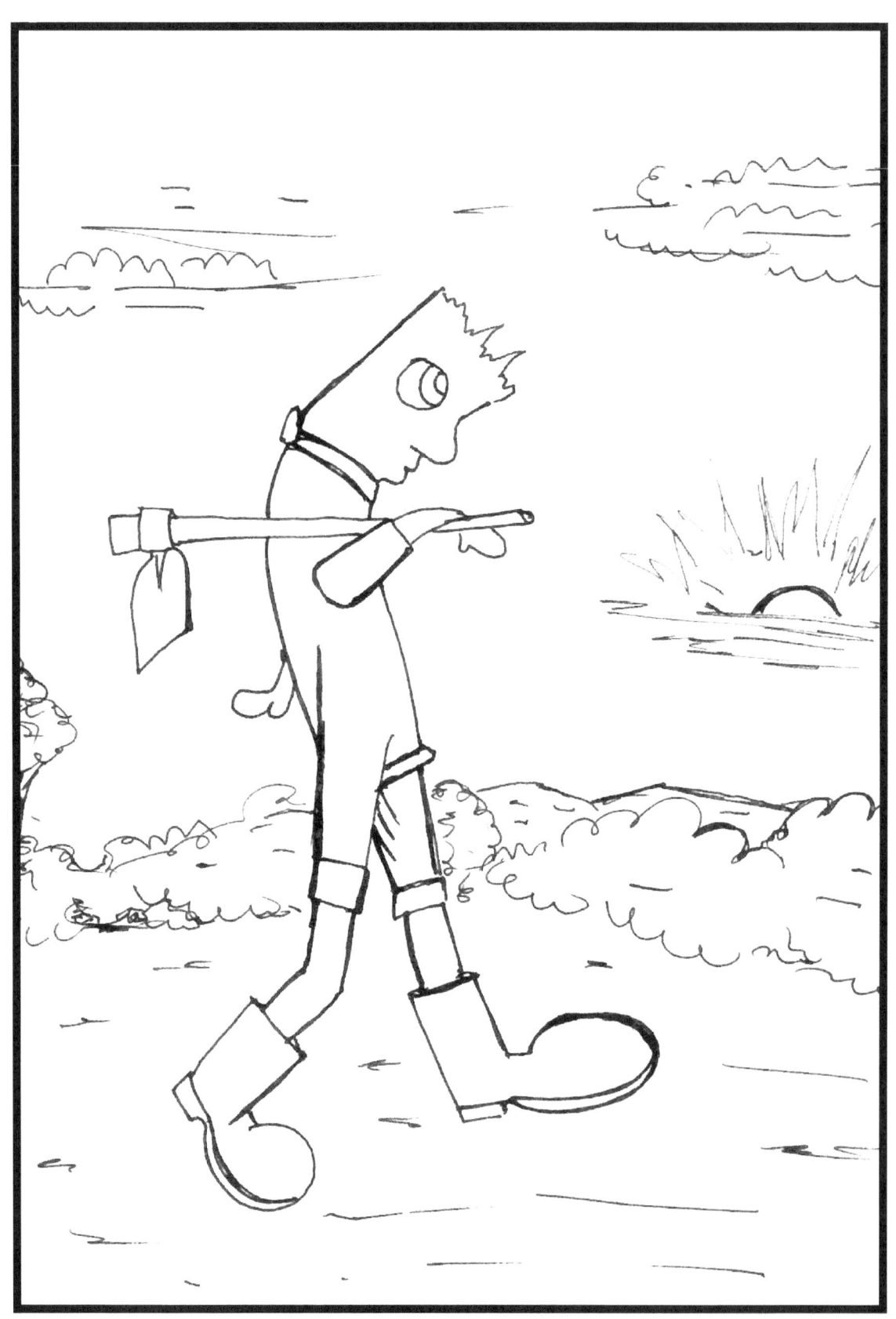

Mr. Hyne is going to dig his garden.

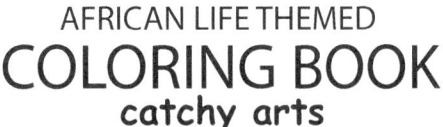

AFRICAN LIFE THEMED
COLORING BOOK
catchy arts

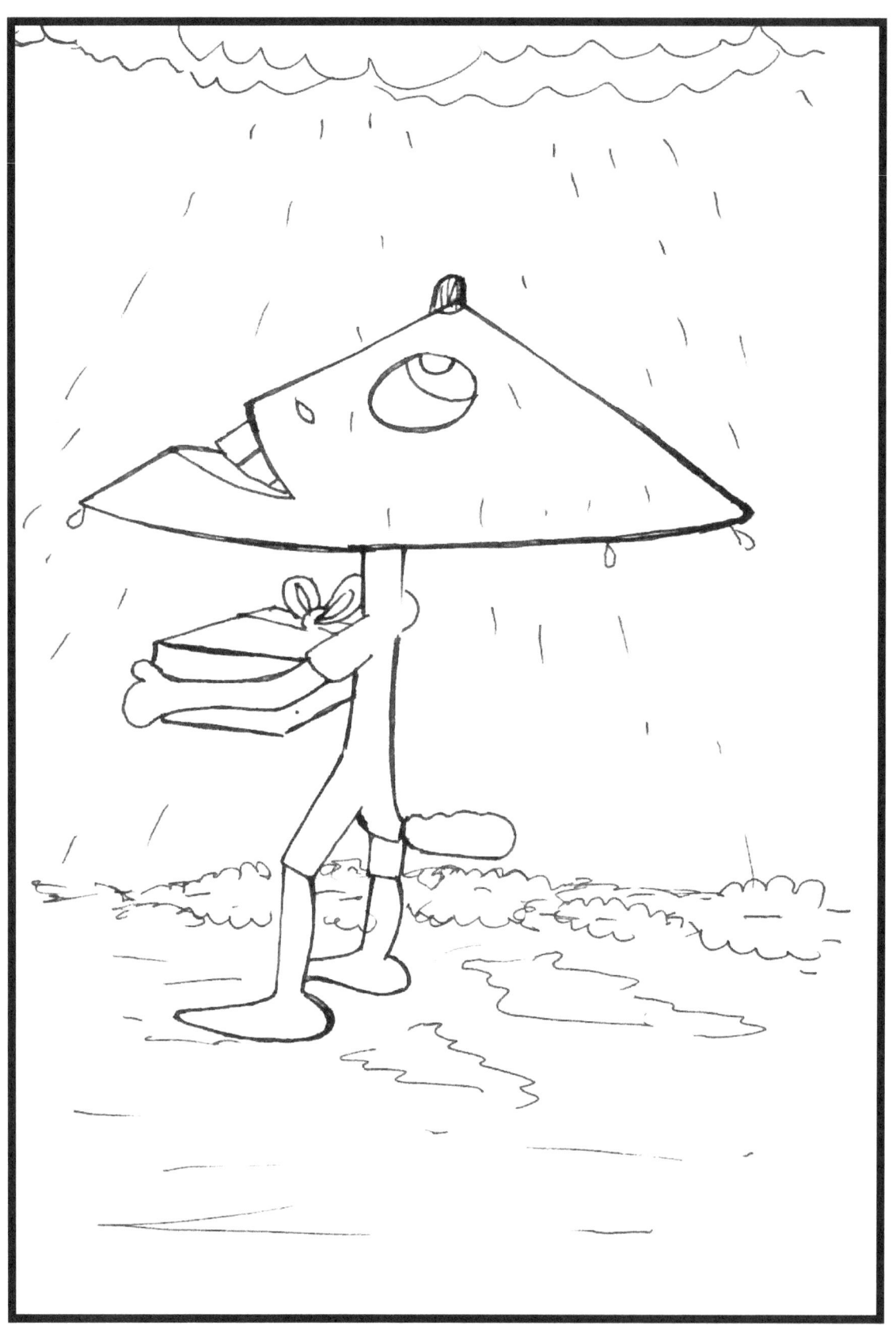

Mr. Umbrella protecting a gift from getting wet

AFRICAN LIFE THEMED
COLORING BOOK
catchy arts
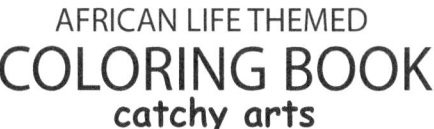

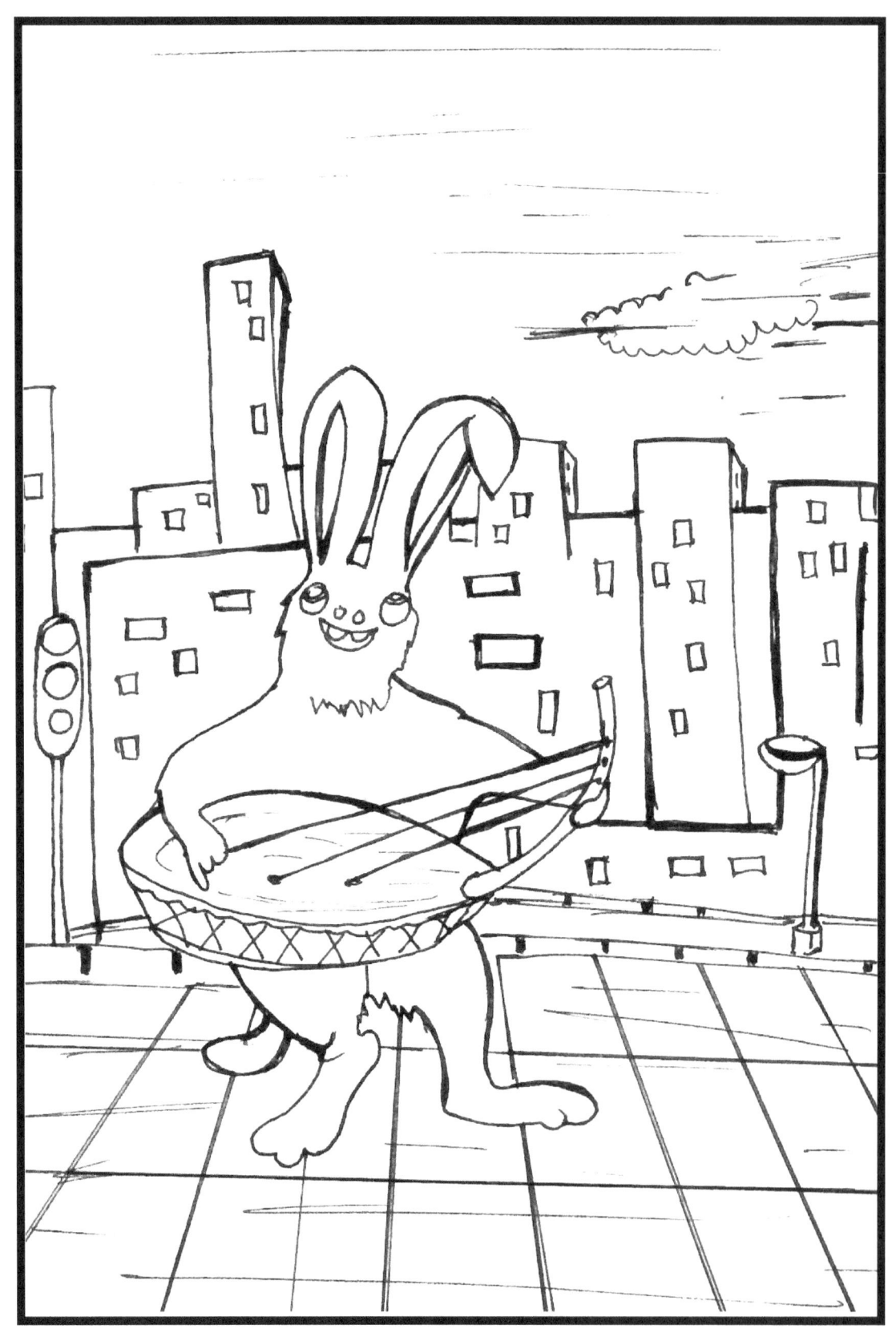

Sir. Rabbit playing a guitar in the city

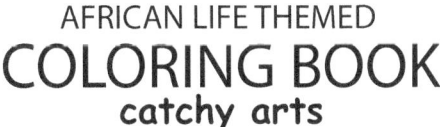

AFRICAN LIFE THEMED
# COLORING BOOK
catchy arts

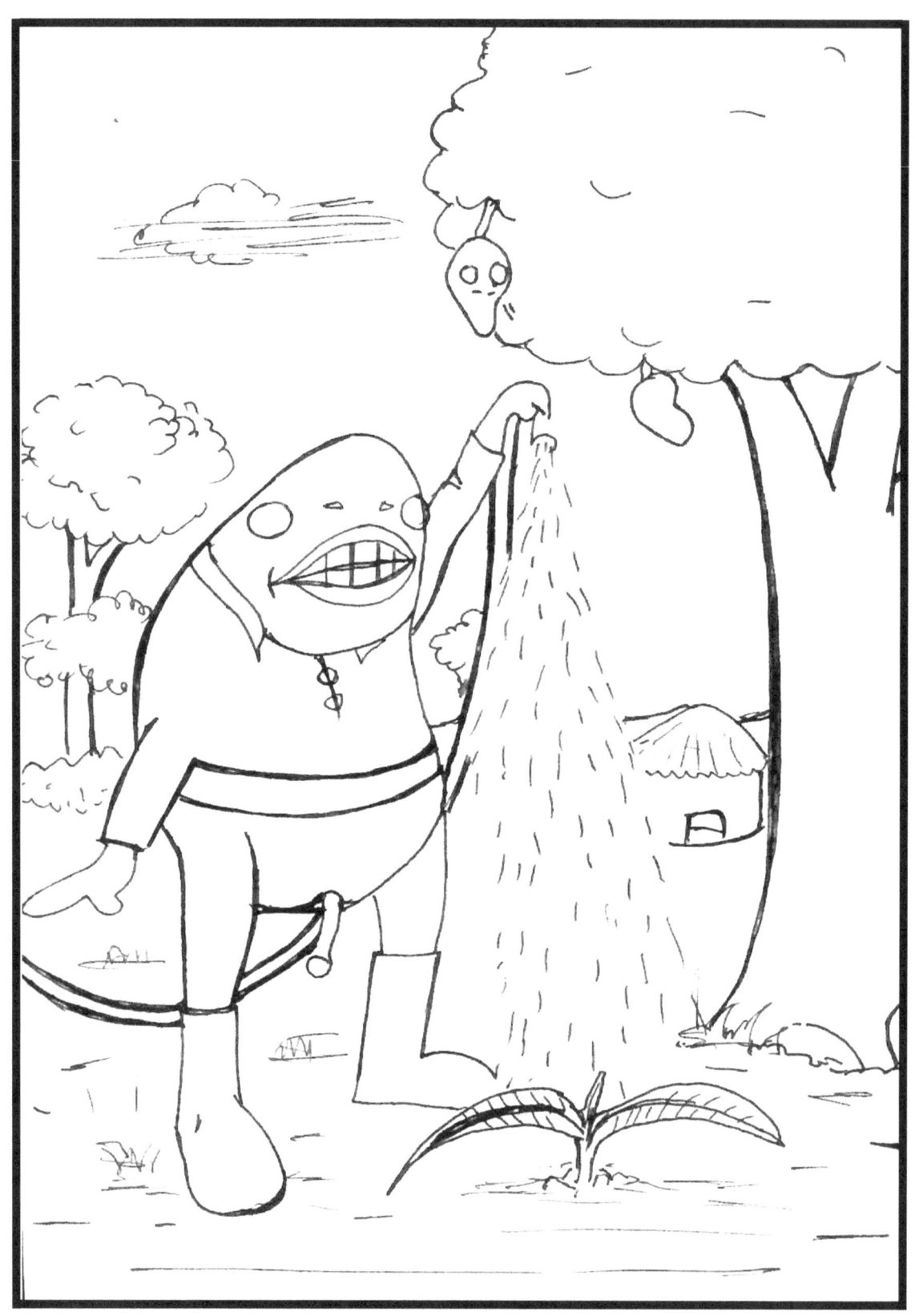

Mr. Mango the farmer is watering a growing flower

AFRICAN LIFE THEMED
# COLORING BOOK
catchy arts

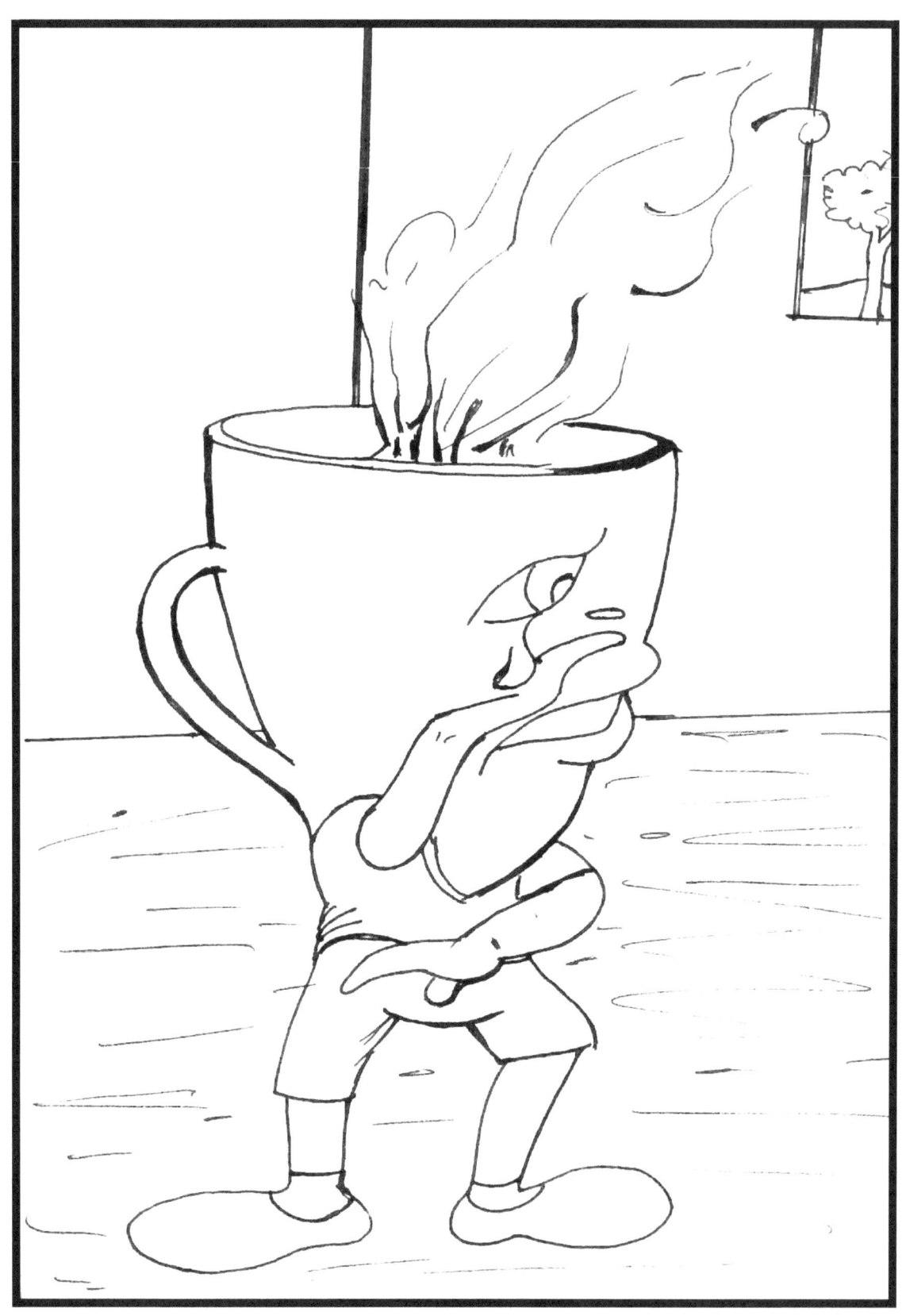

Mr. James the cup crying because of hot water.

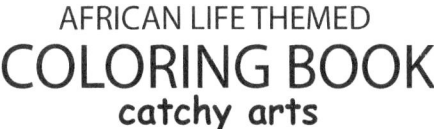

AFRICAN LIFE THEMED
# COLORING BOOK
catchy arts

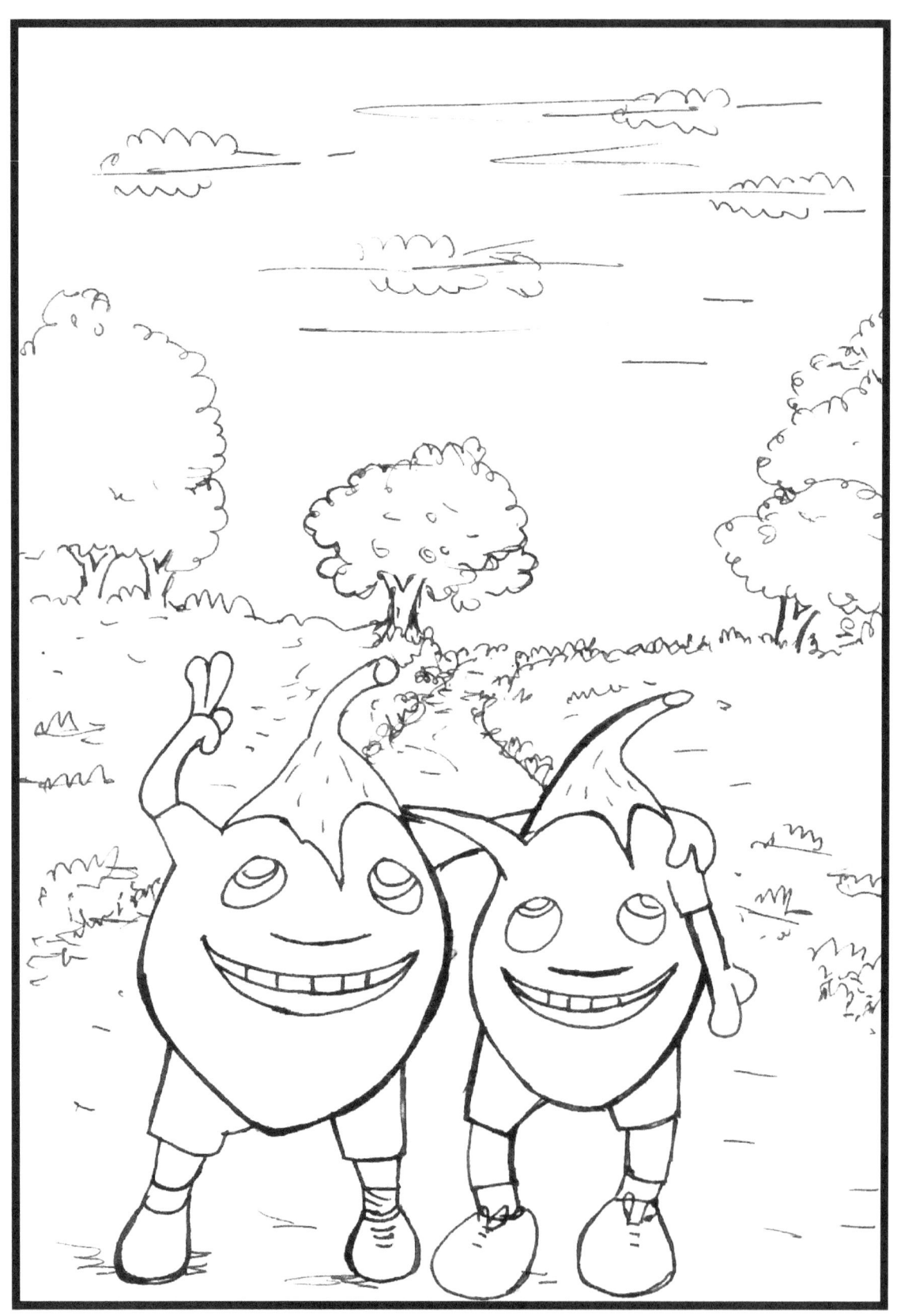

Two beautiful egg plants engoying the walk

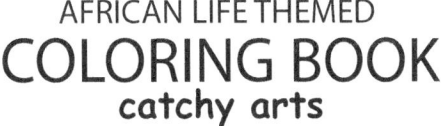

AFRICAN LIFE THEMED
COLORING BOOK
catchy arts

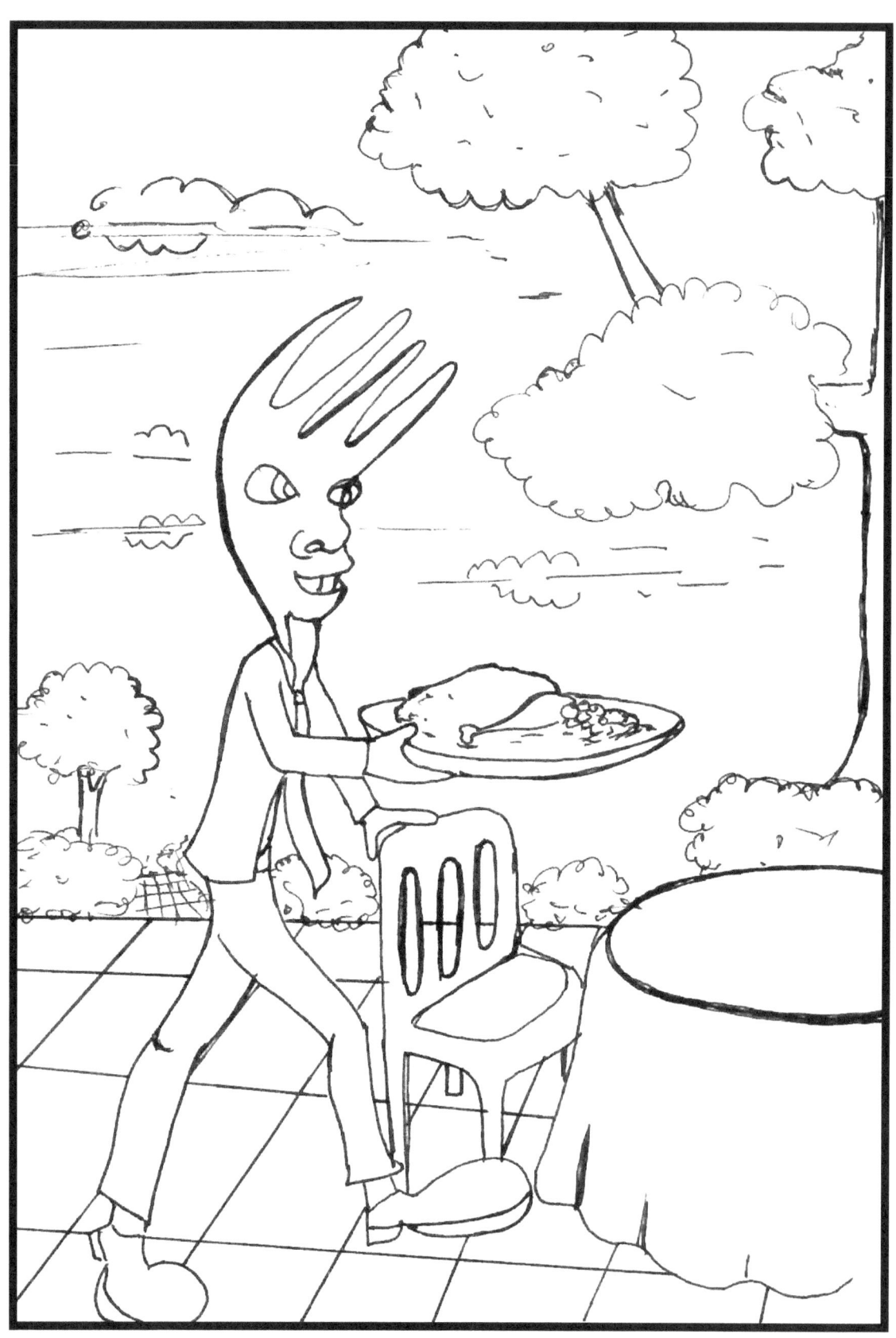

A brave fork serving food.

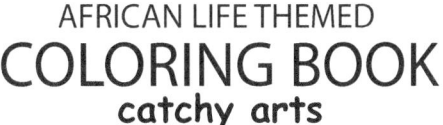

AFRICAN LIFE THEMED
COLORING BOOK
catchy arts

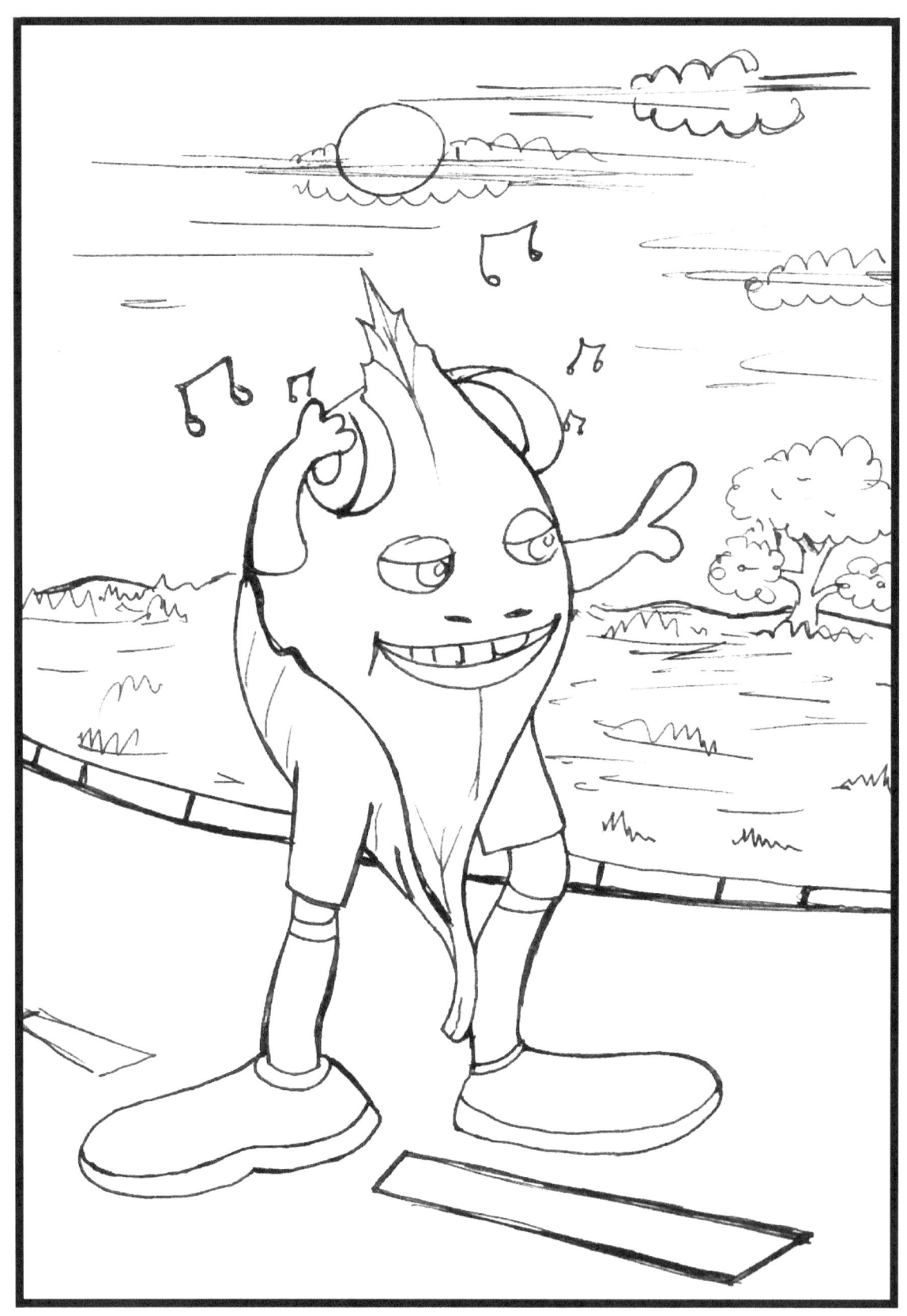

A leaf listening to music

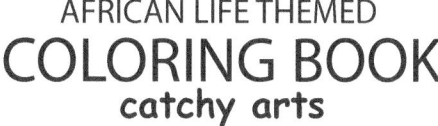

AFRICAN LIFE THEMED
COLORING BOOK
catchy arts

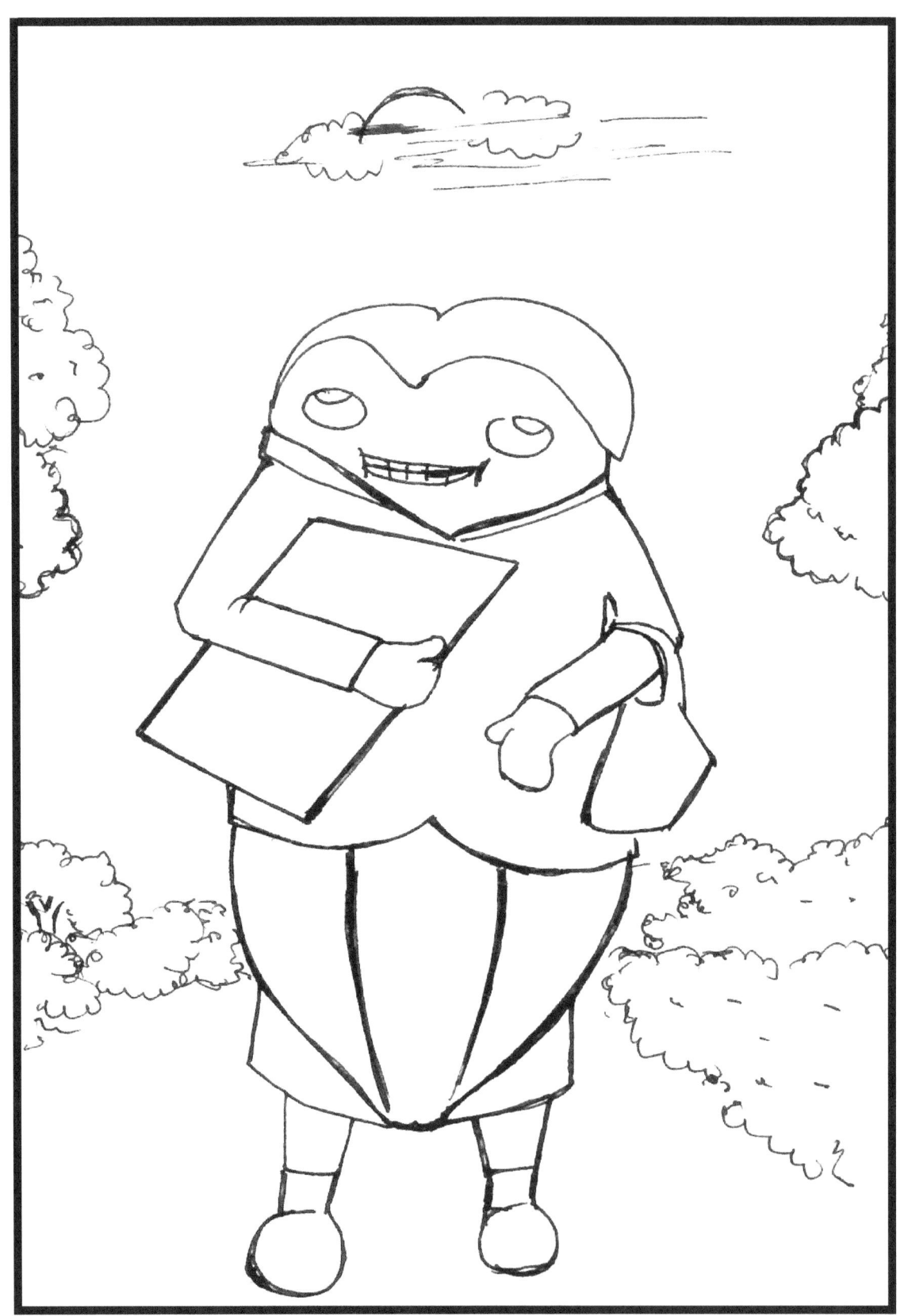

Madam pawpaw going to her office

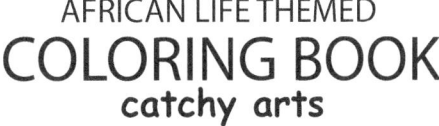

AFRICAN LIFE THEMED
COLORING BOOK
catchy arts

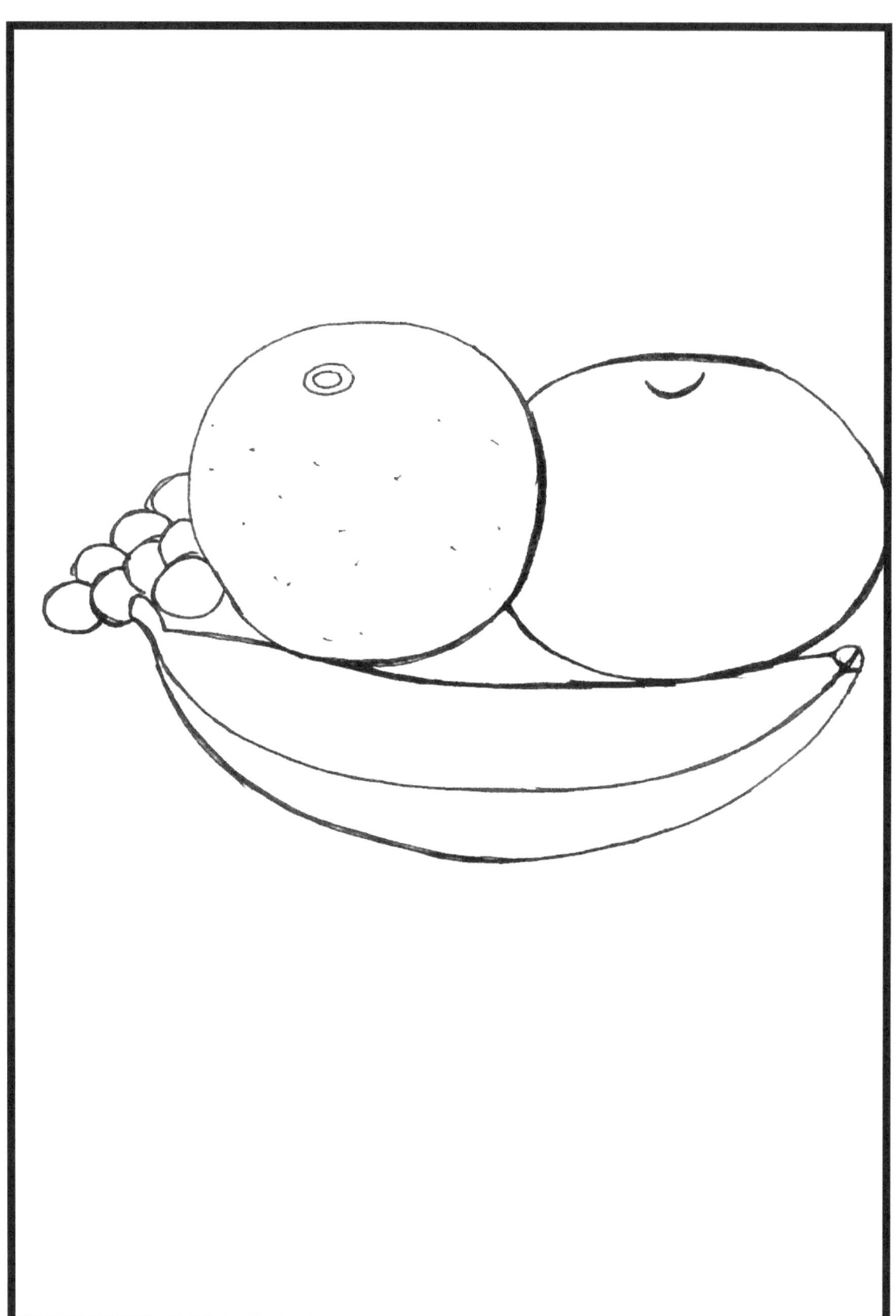

Sweet fruits

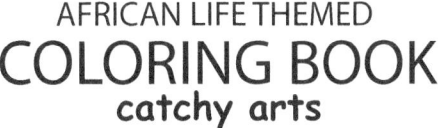

AFRICAN LIFE THEMED
# COLORING BOOK
catchy arts

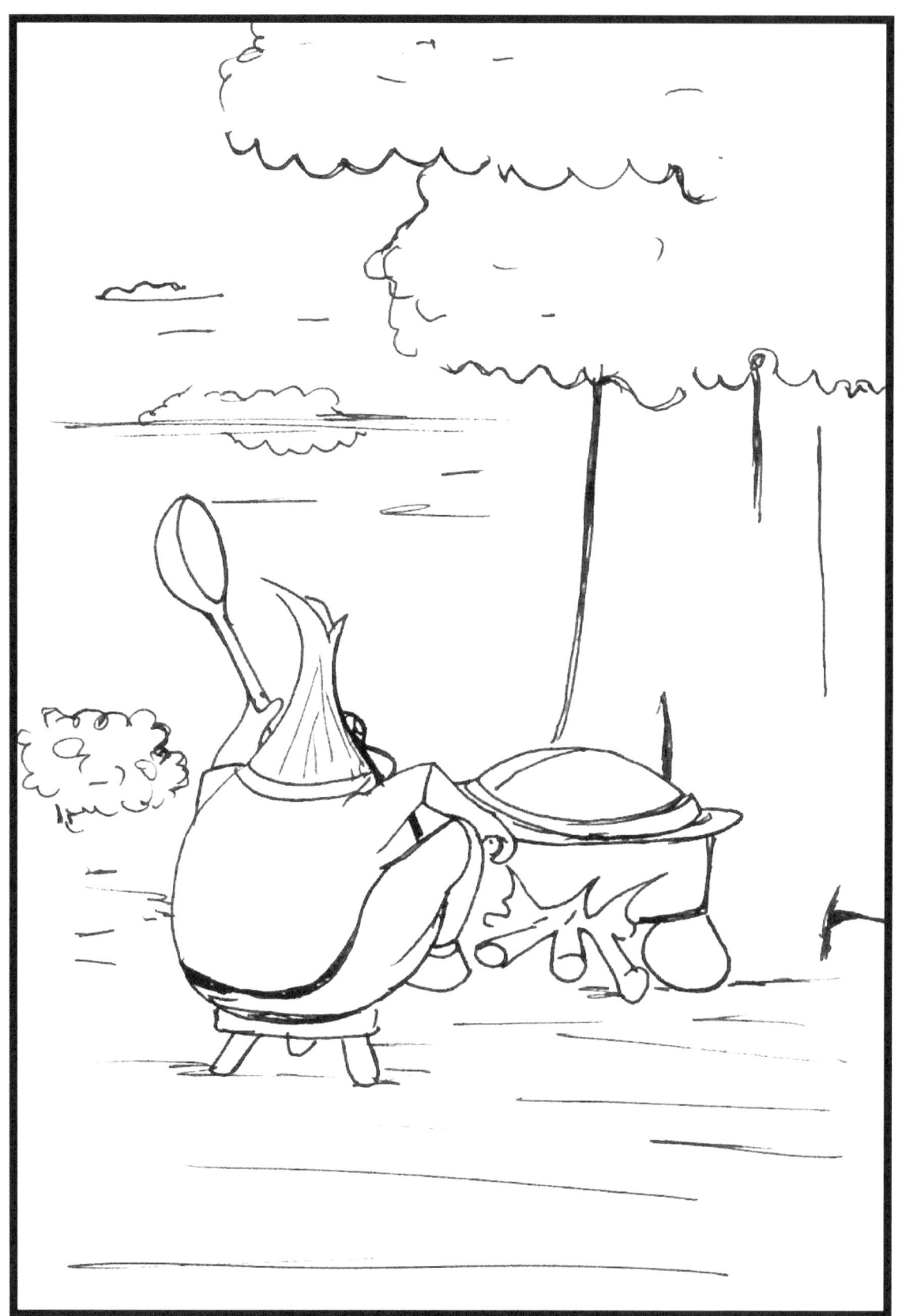

Mr. Onion ccoking.

AFRICAN LIFE THEMED
# COLORING BOOK
catchy arts

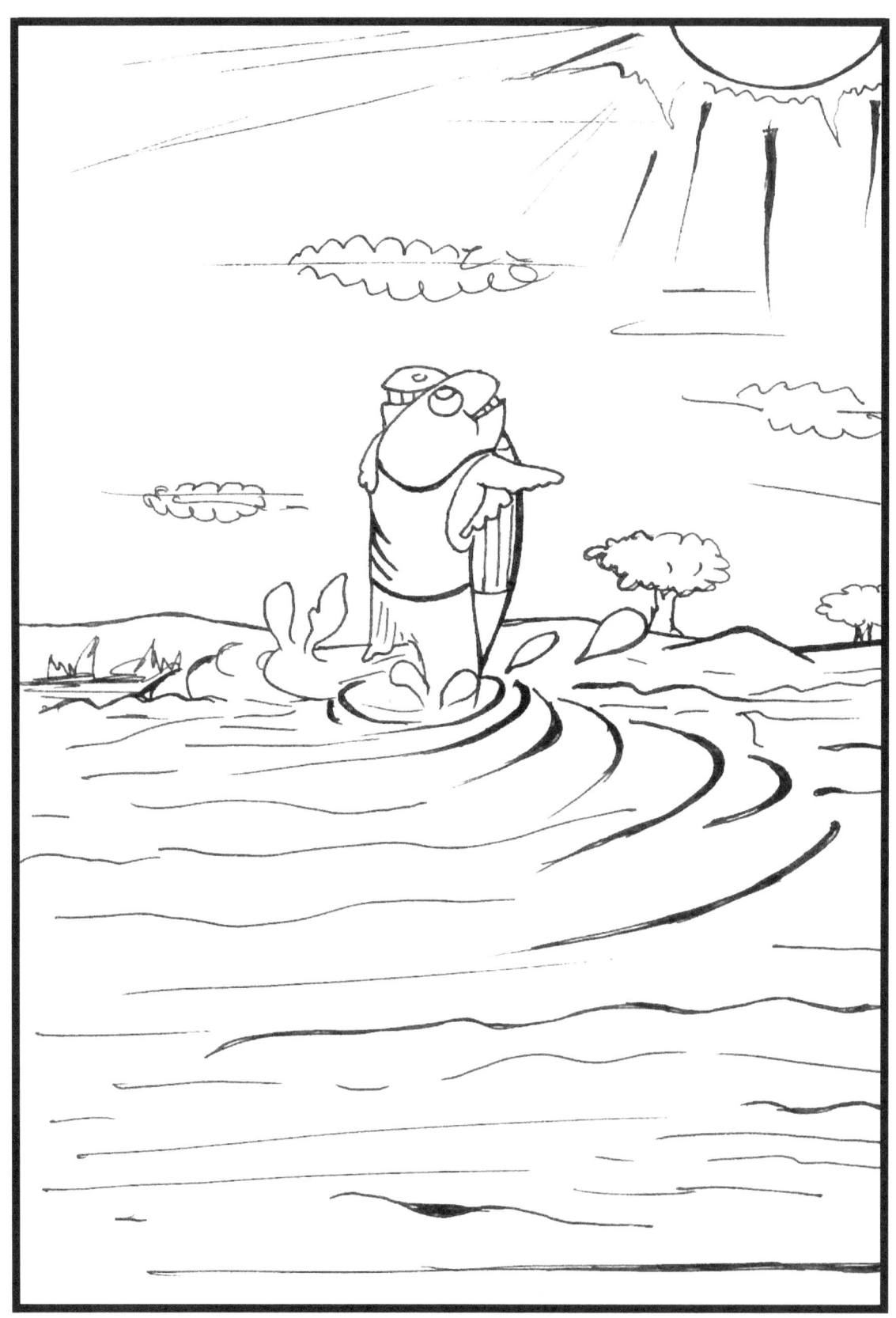

Two fish enjoying a hug in ocean water

AFRICAN LIFE THEMED
# COLORING BOOK
catchy arts

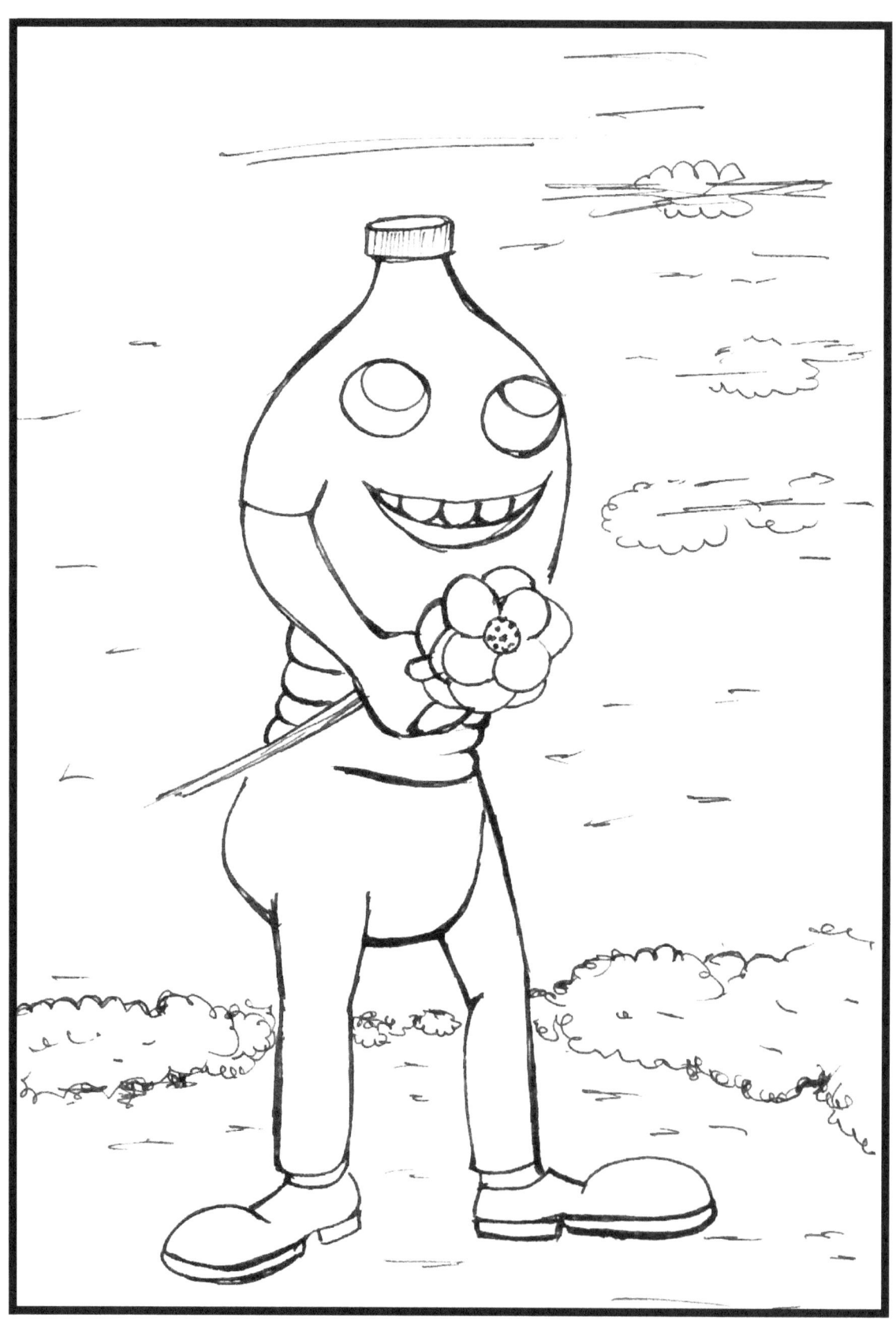

Mr. Bottle holding a flower

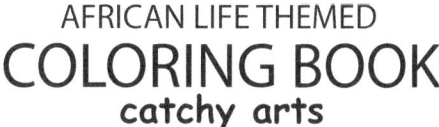

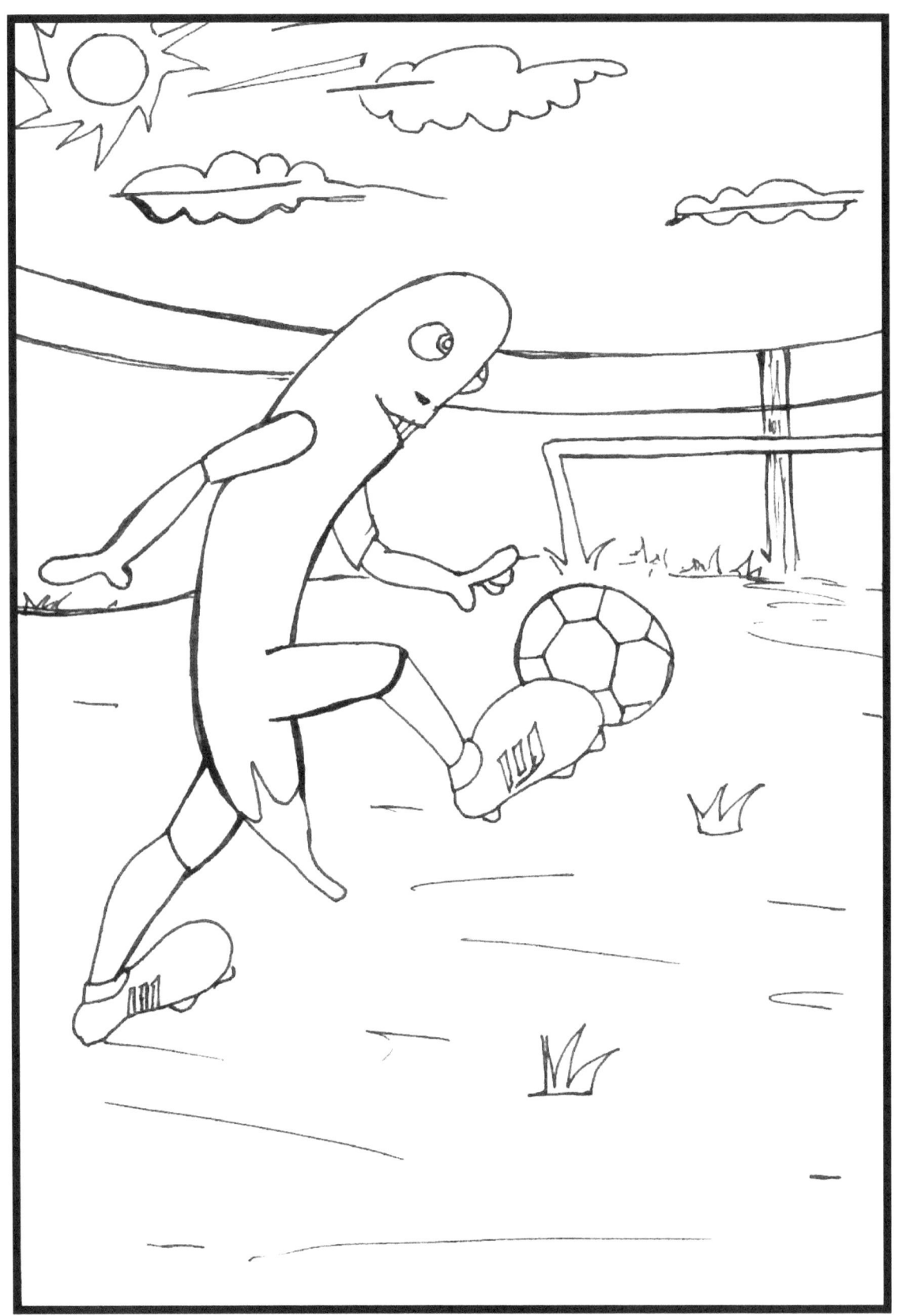

Mr. Eggplant playing soccer

AFRICAN LIFE THEMED
# COLORING BOOK
catchy arts

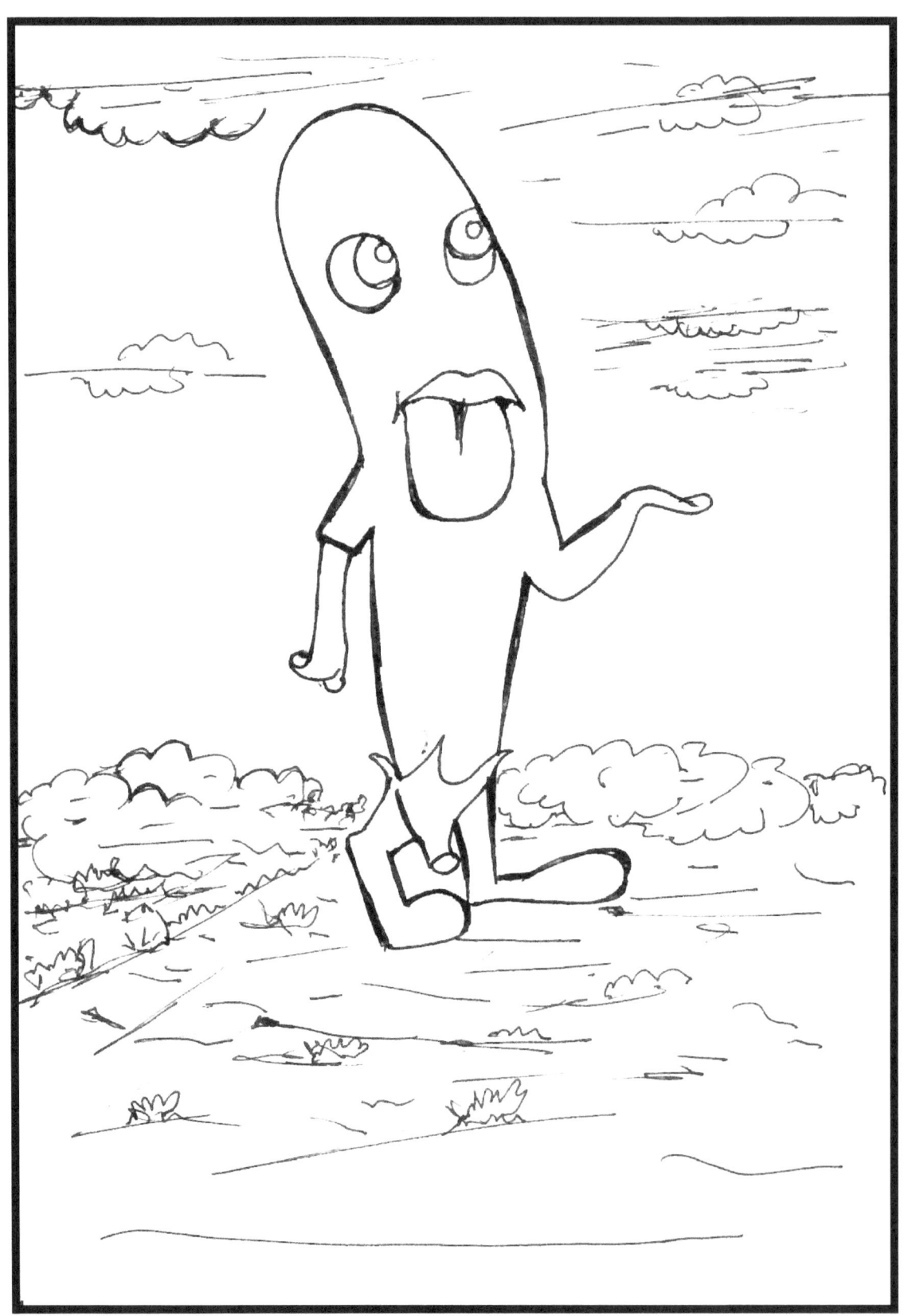

Mr. Egg plant dancing.

AFRICAN LIFE THEMED
COLORING BOOK
catchy arts

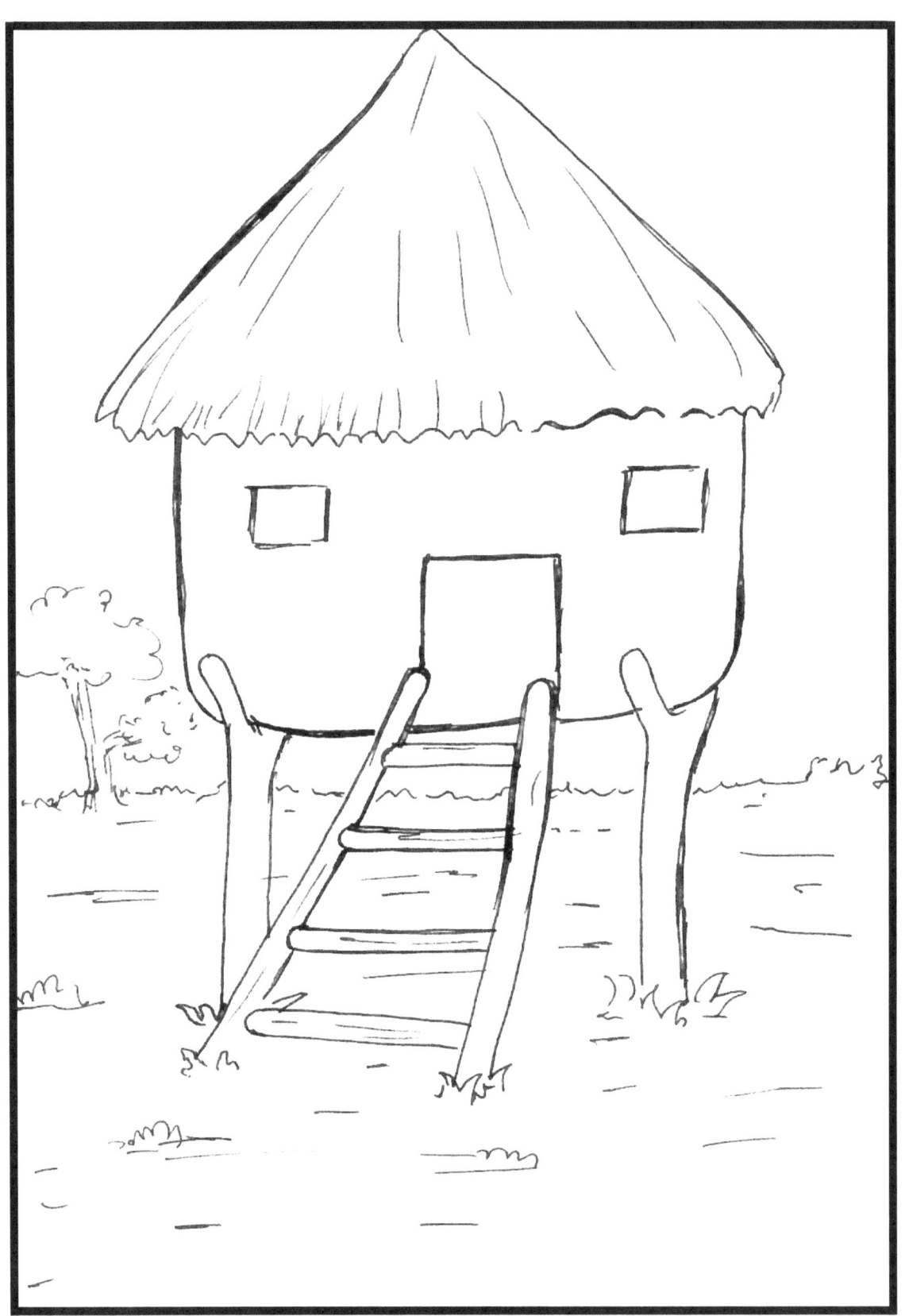

Asante's home.

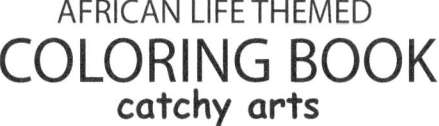

AFRICAN LIFE THEMED
COLORING BOOK
catchy arts

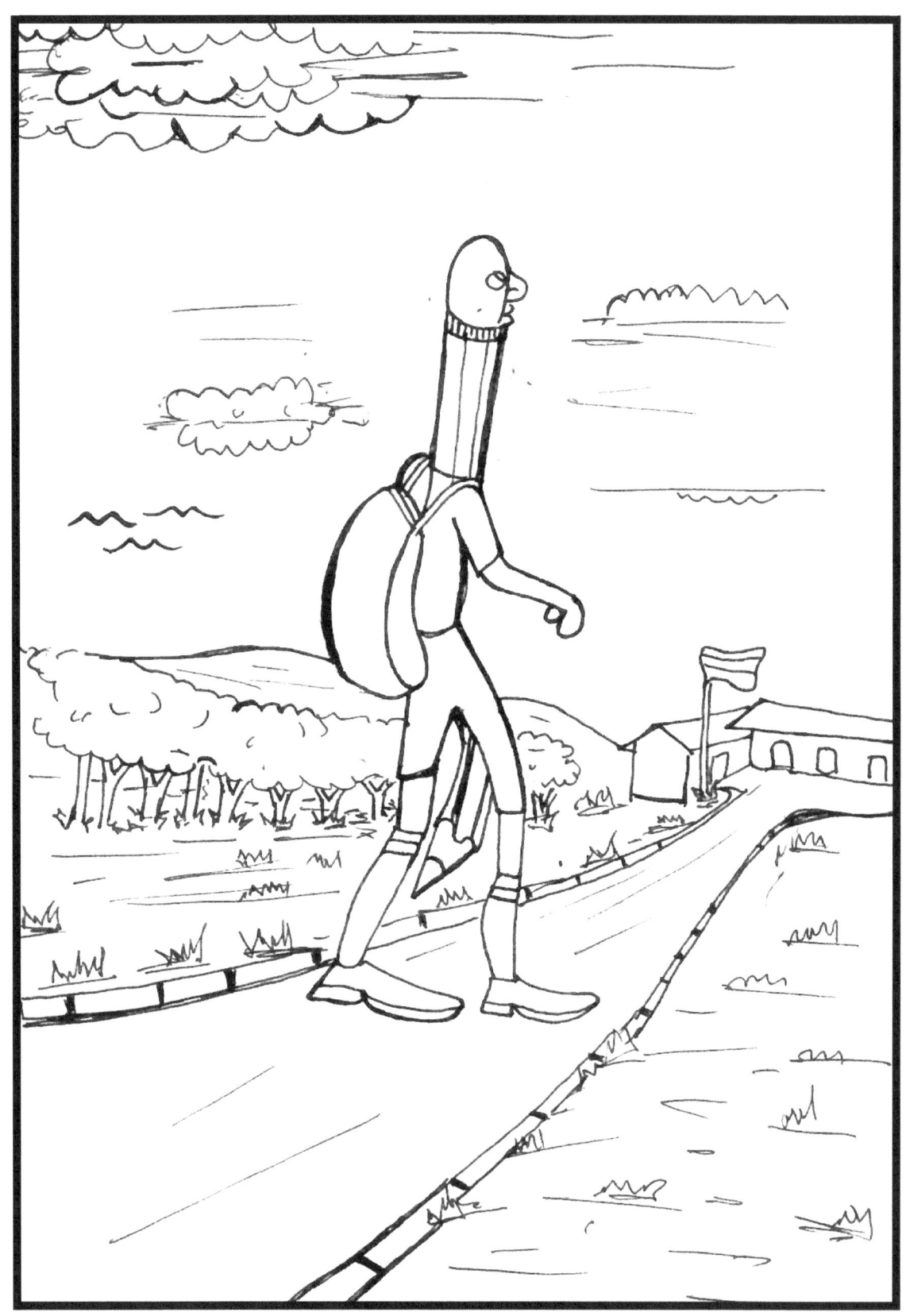

Baby pencil going to school.

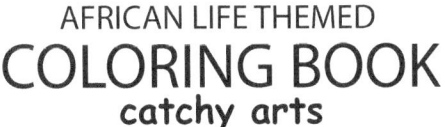

AFRICAN LIFE THEMED
COLORING BOOK
catchy arts

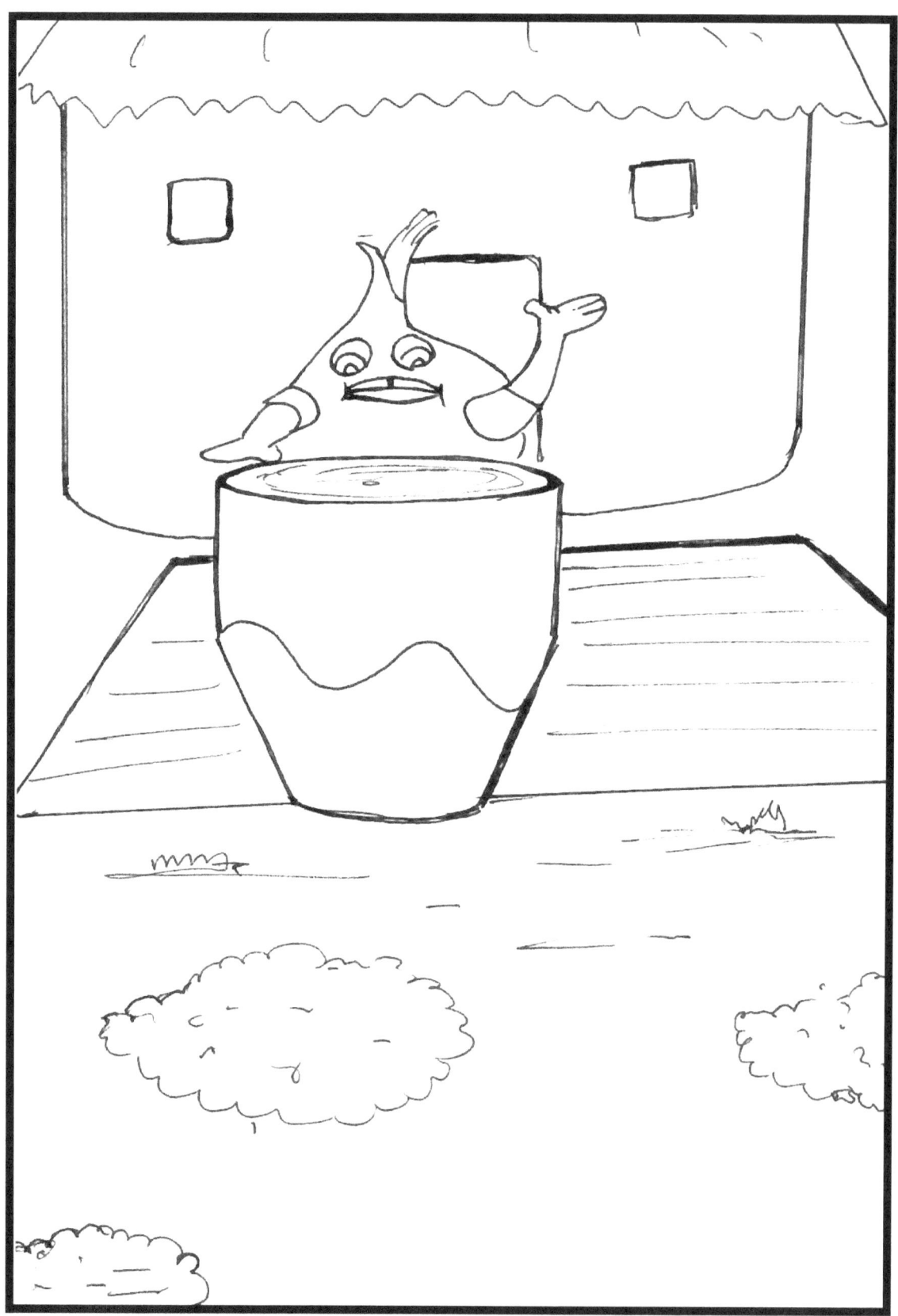

Mr. Onion druming

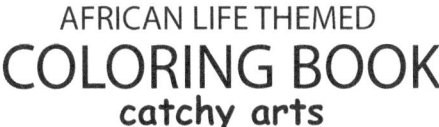

AFRICAN LIFE THEMED
COLORING BOOK
catchy arts

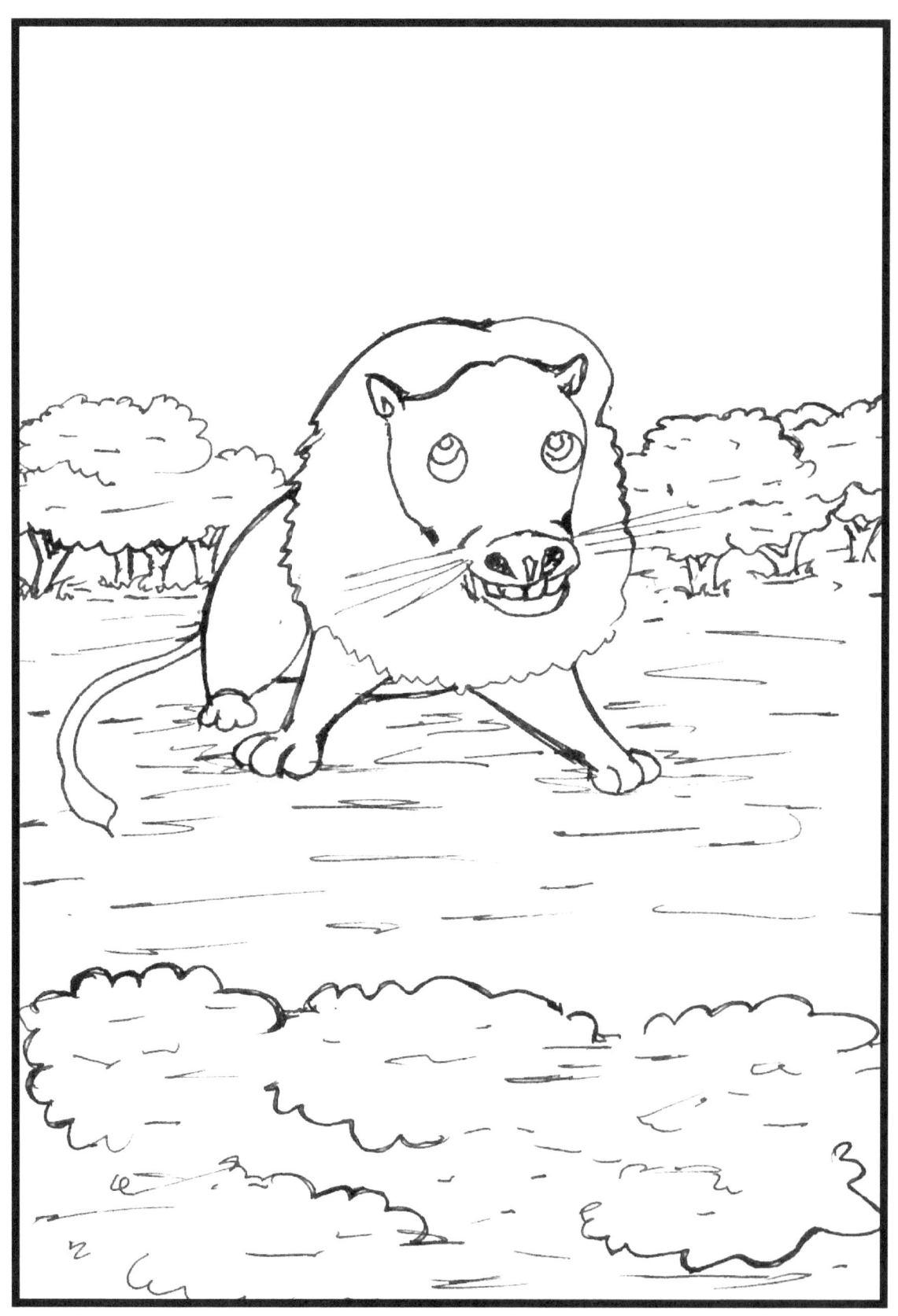

Mr. Lion in the bush

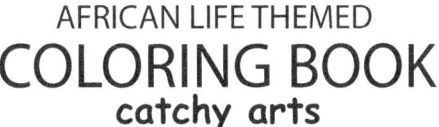
AFRICAN LIFE THEMED
COLORING BOOK
catchy arts

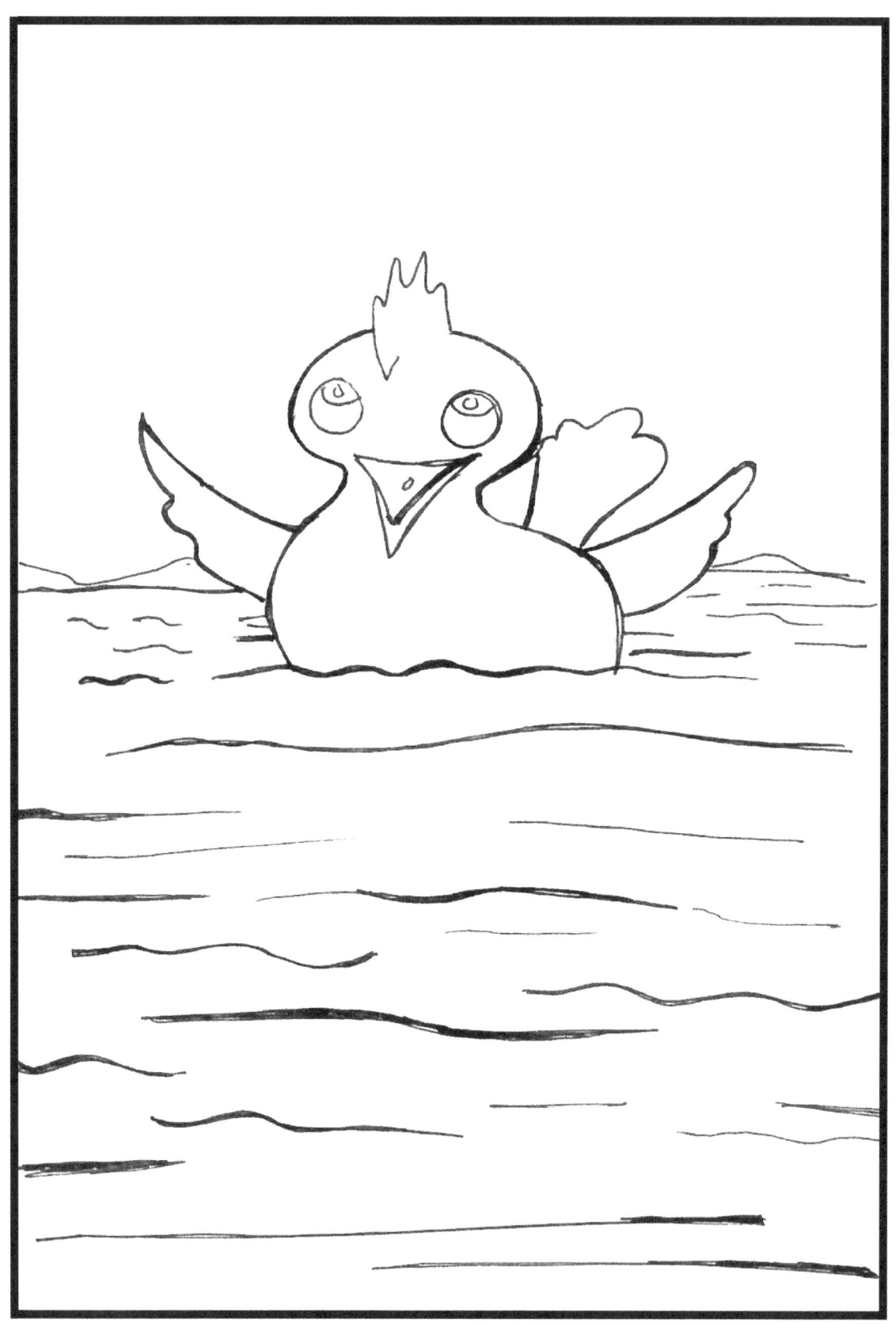

Mr. Duck swimming

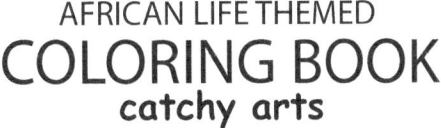

AFRICAN LIFE THEMED
COLORING BOOK
catchy arts

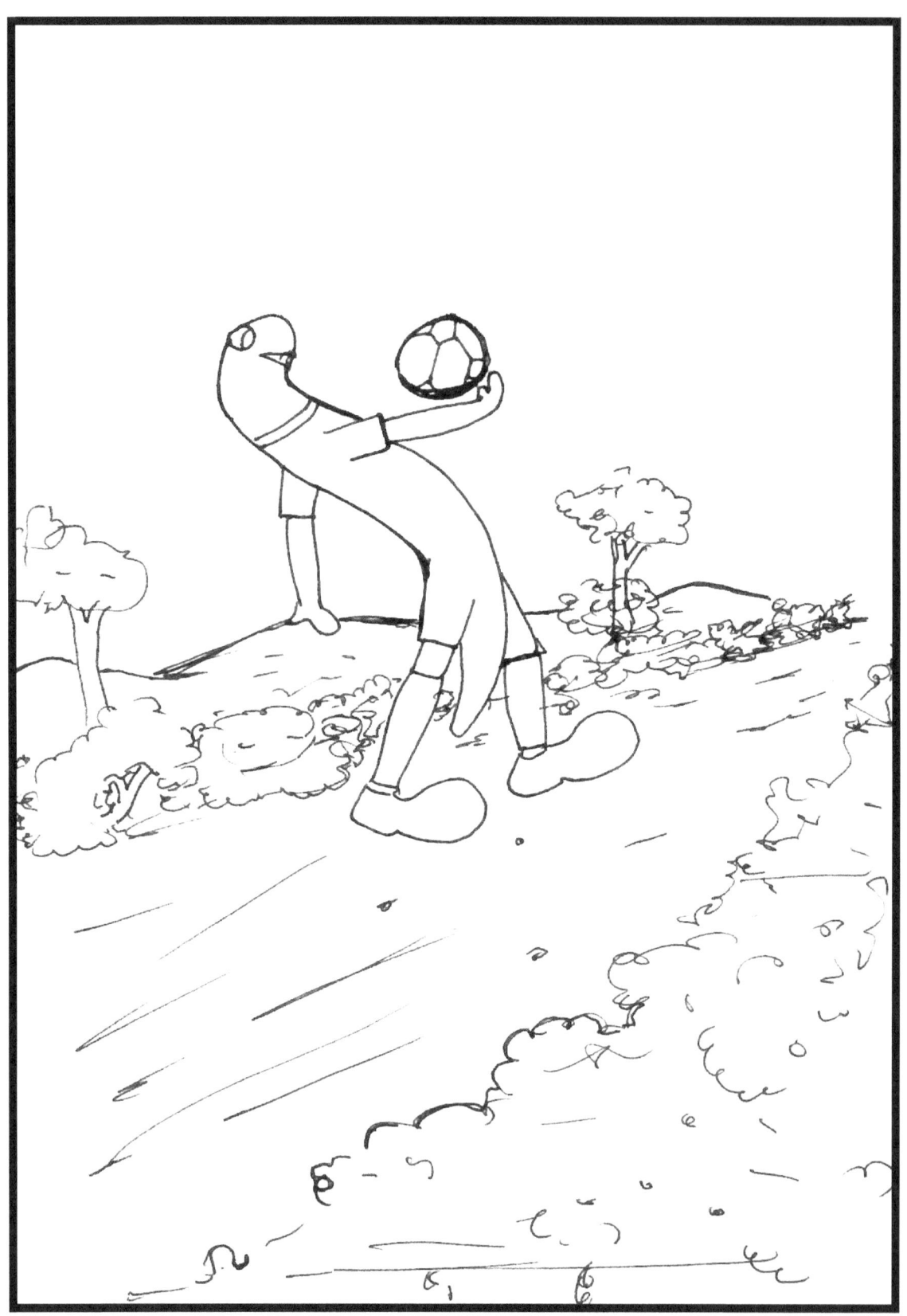

A snake playing with the ball

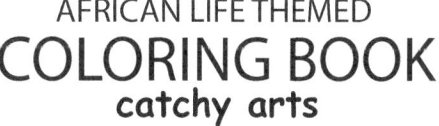

AFRICAN LIFE THEMED
COLORING BOOK
catchy arts

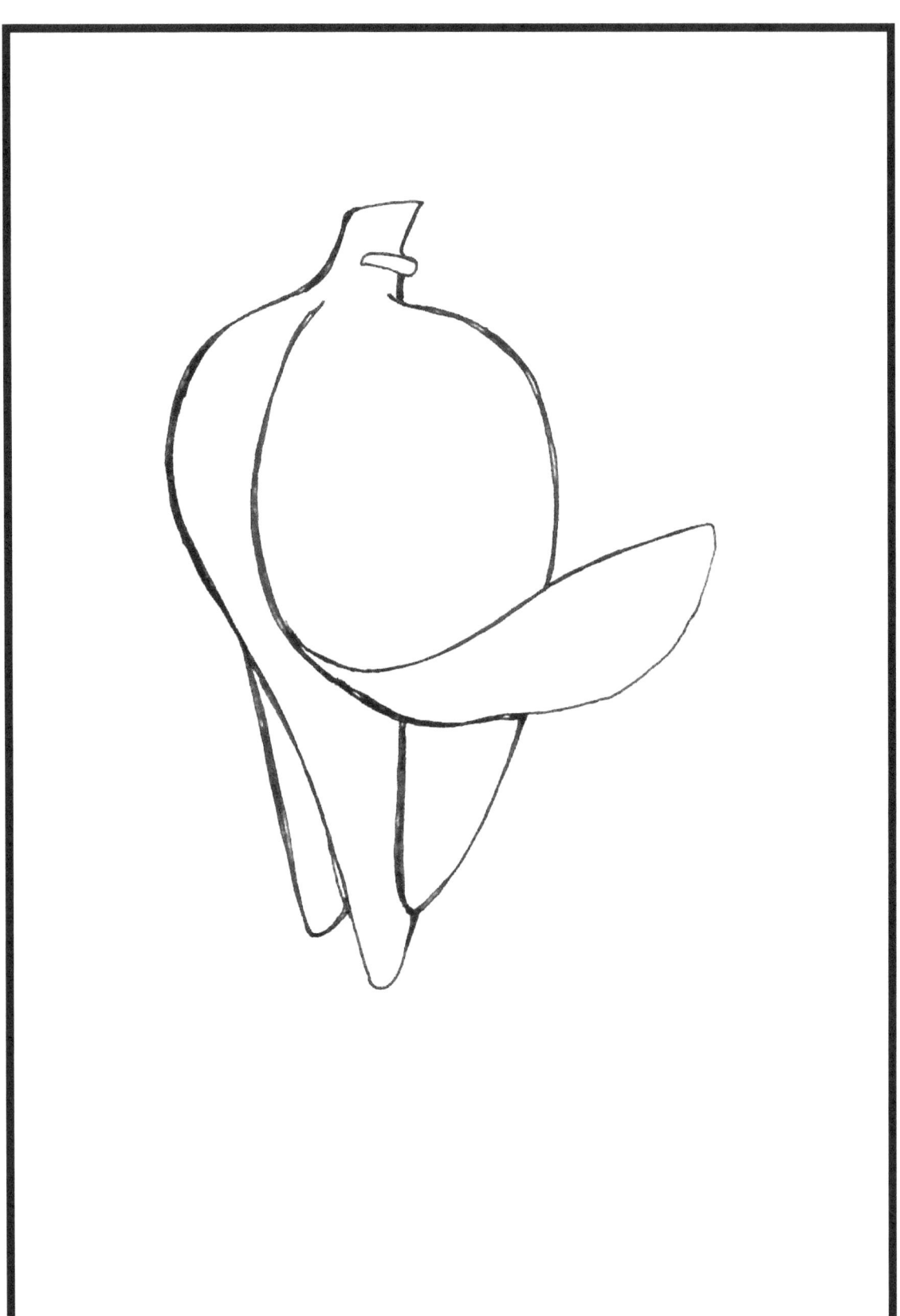

Banana flower,

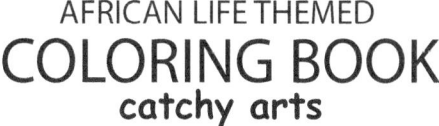

AFRICAN LIFE THEMED
COLORING BOOK
catchy arts

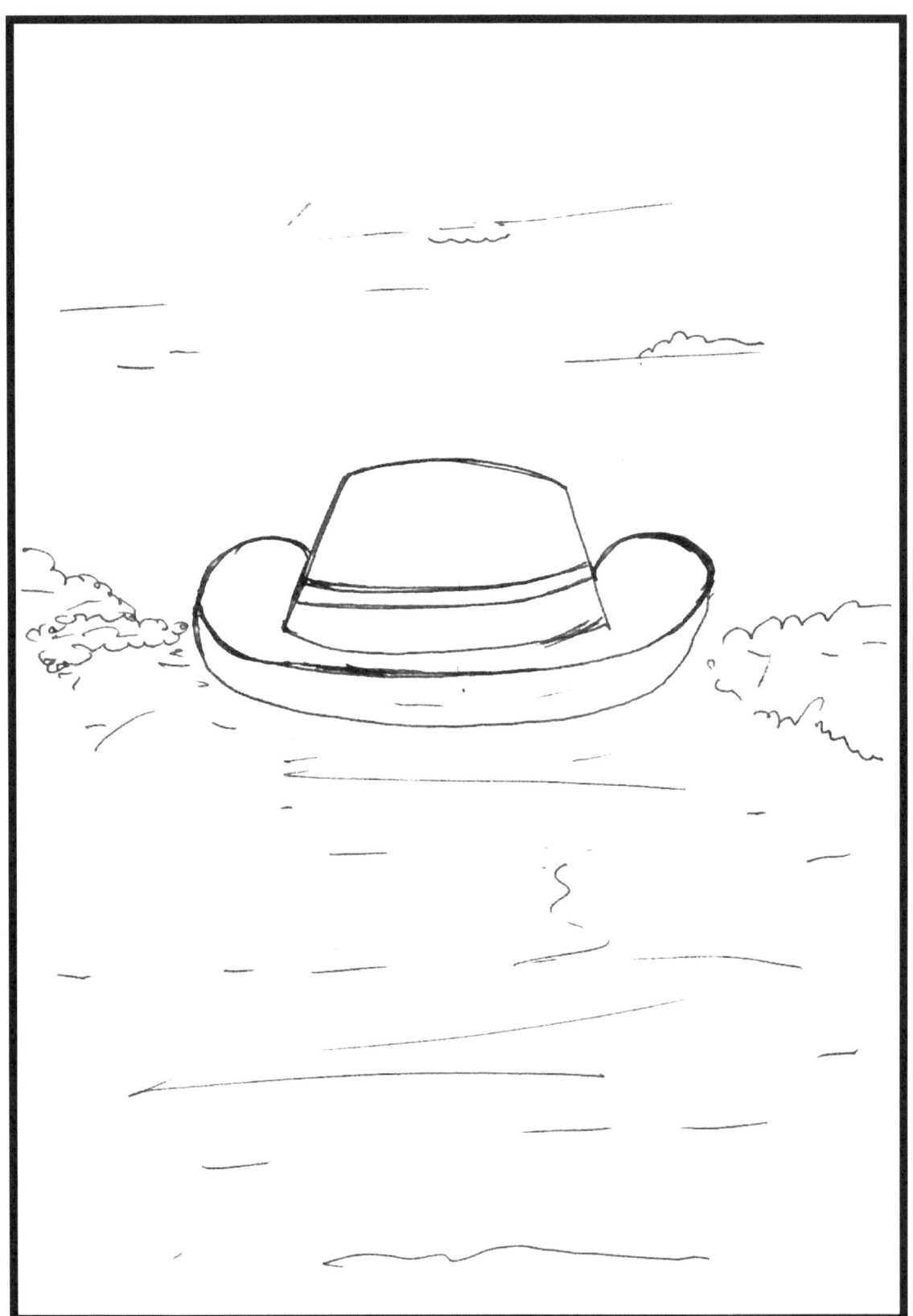

The hat

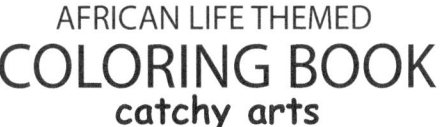

AFRICAN LIFE THEMED
COLORING BOOK
catchy arts

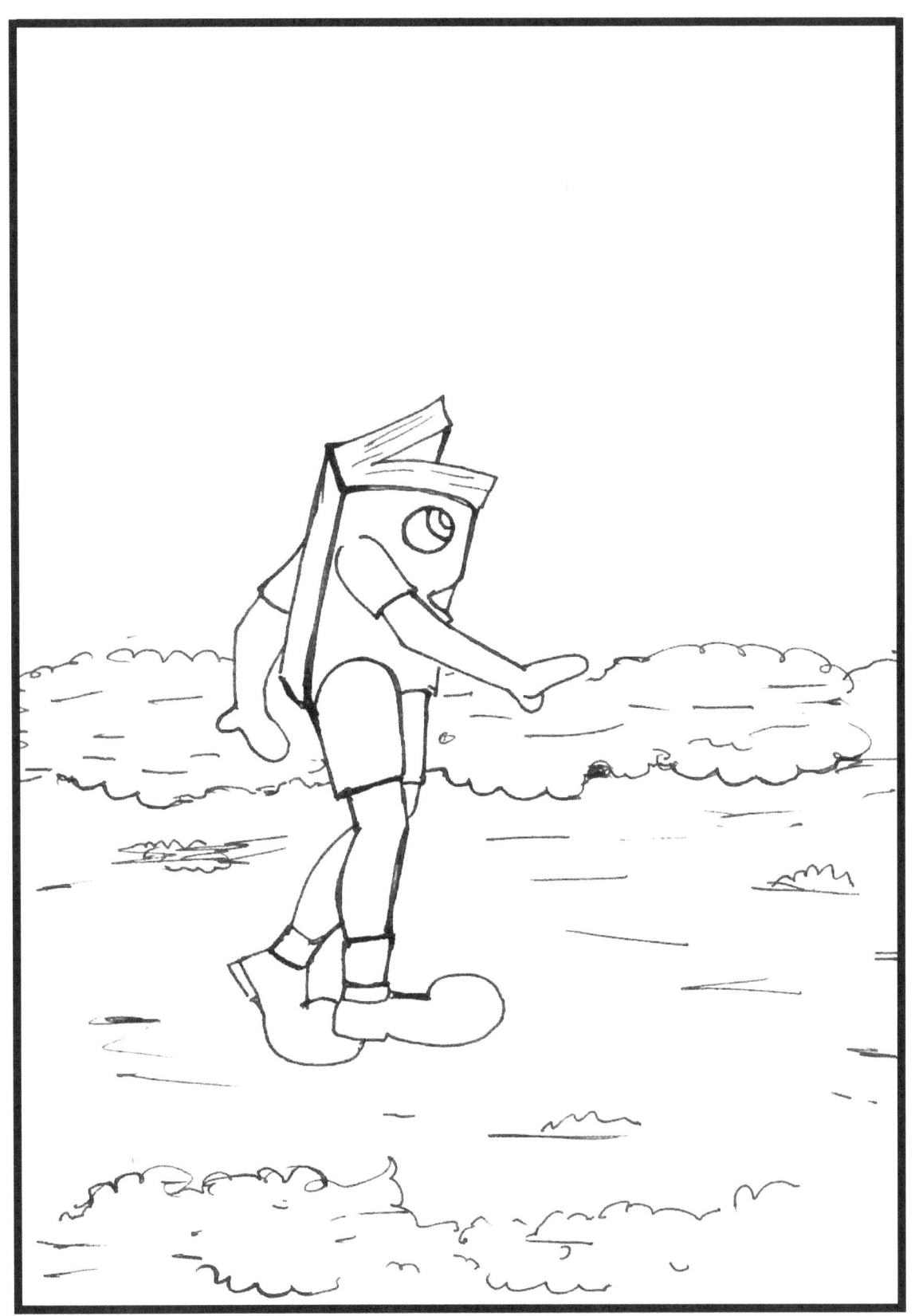

Mr. Book walkimg

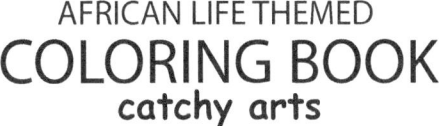

AFRICAN LIFE THEMED
COLORING BOOK
catchy arts

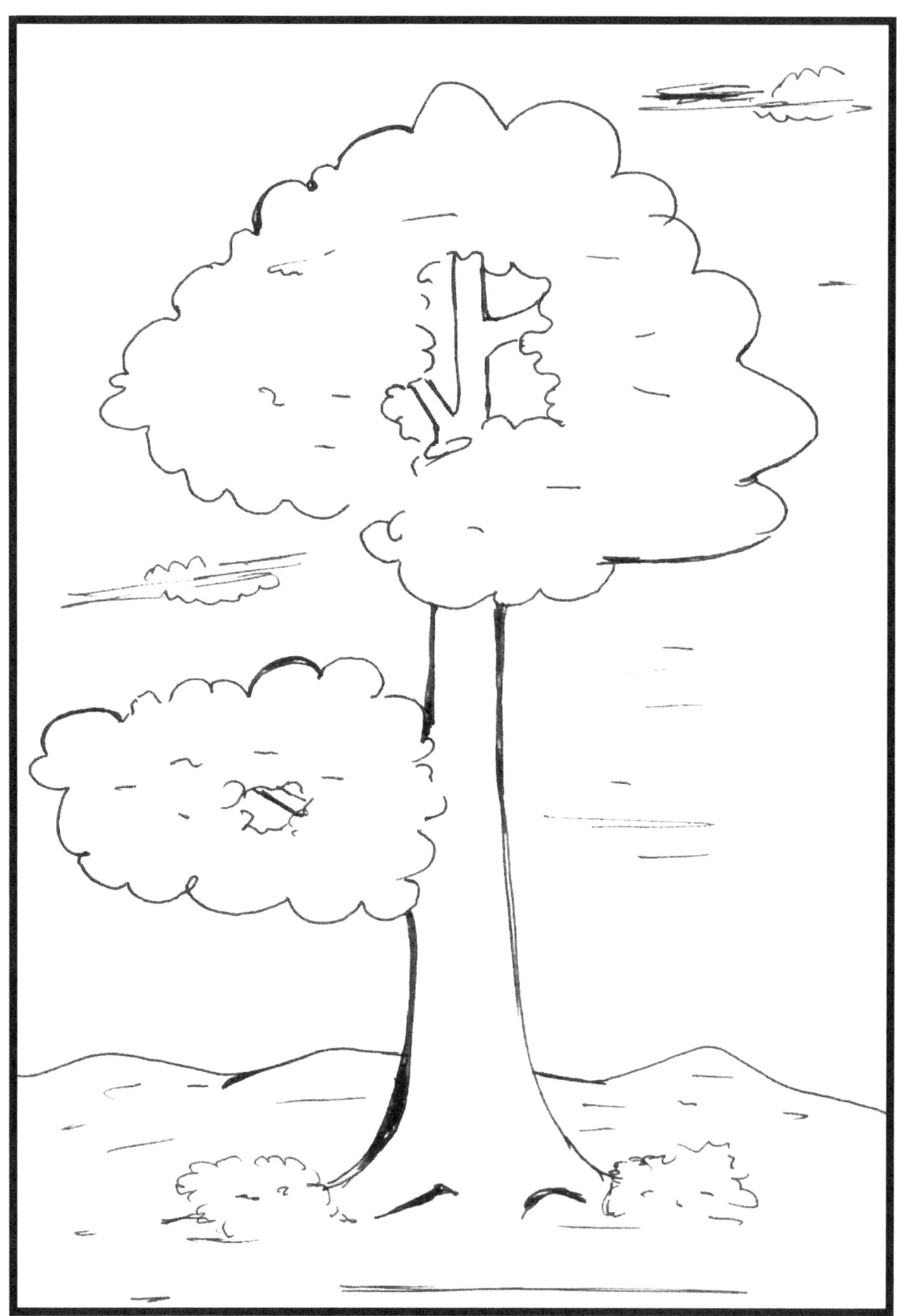

A tree

AFRICAN LIFE THEMED
# COLORING BOOK
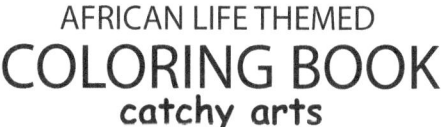

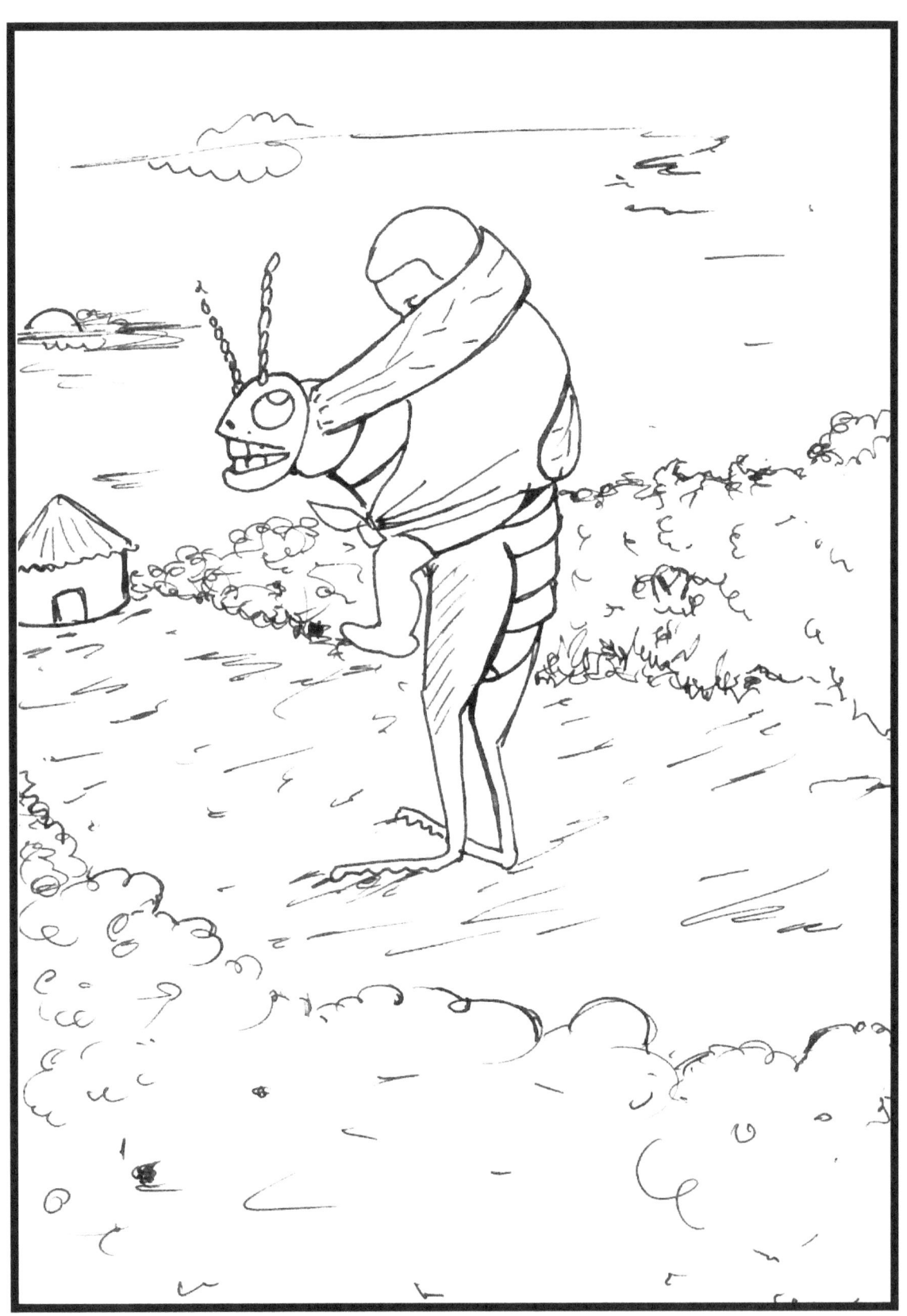

A grasshopper carrying a baby

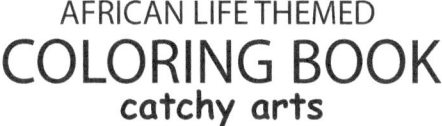

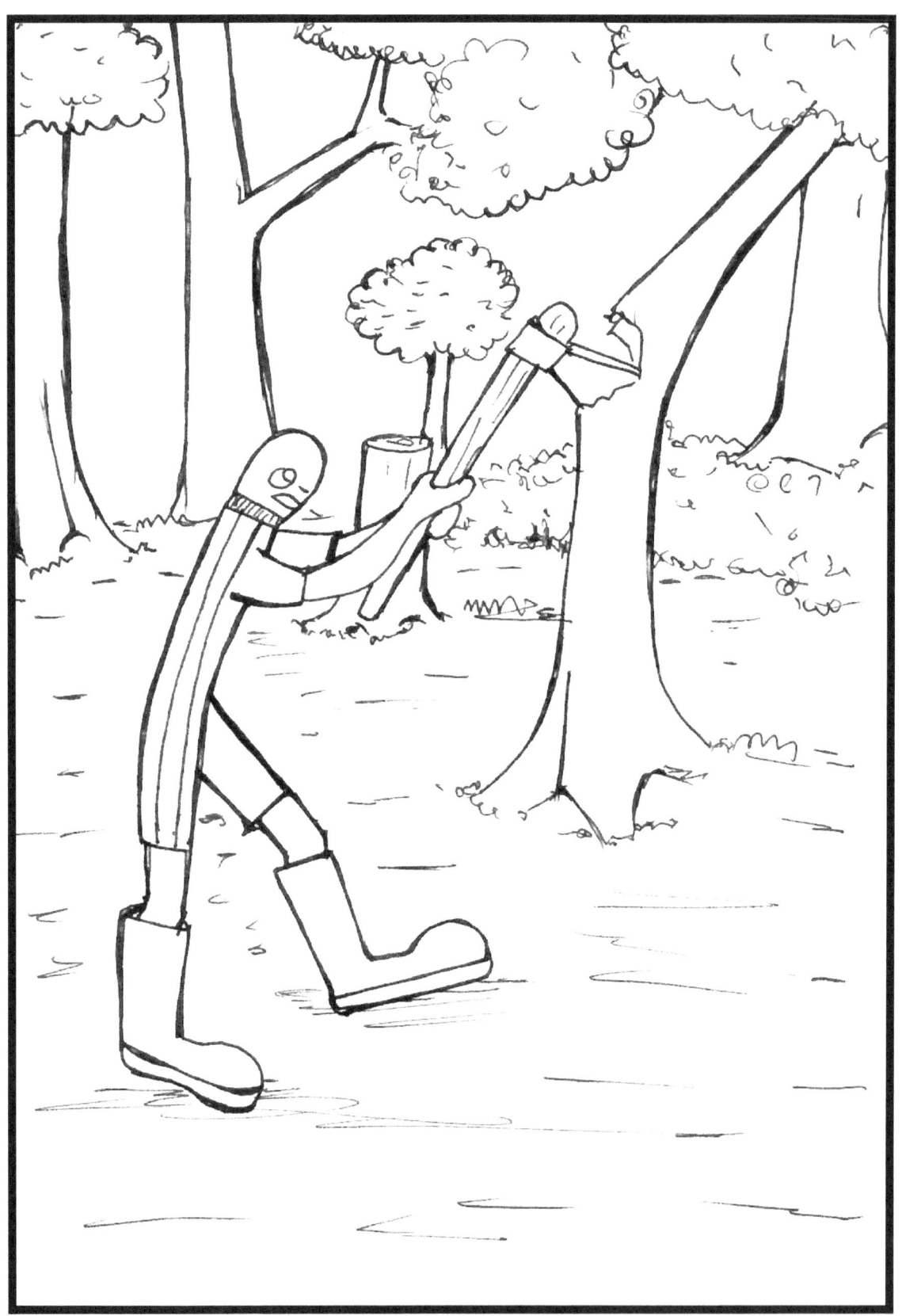

Mr. Snake cutting the tree

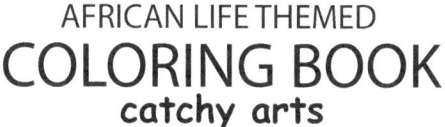

AFRICAN LIFE THEMED
COLORING BOOK
catchy arts

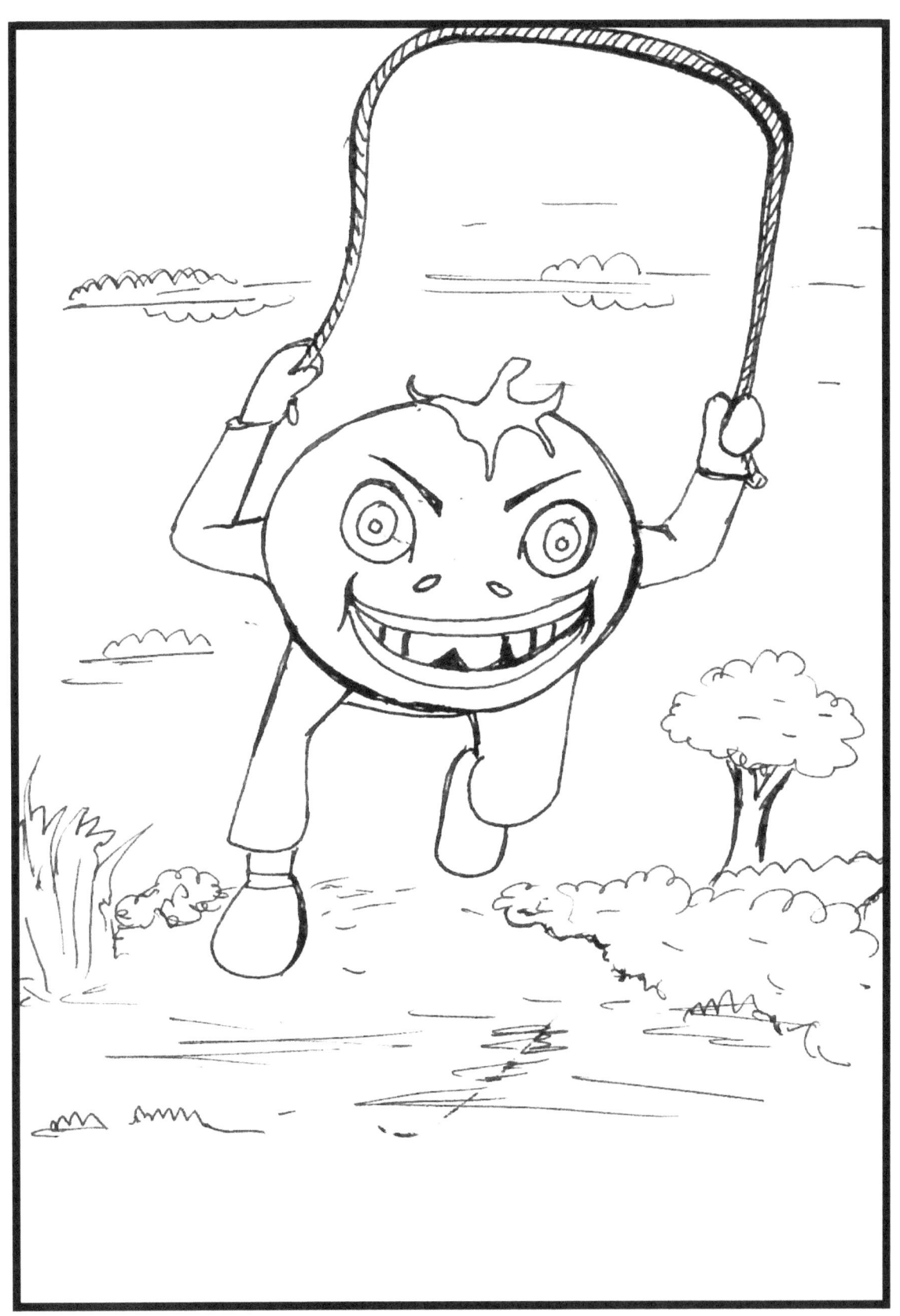

Baby water melon playing

AFRICAN LIFE THEMED
COLORING BOOK
catchy arts

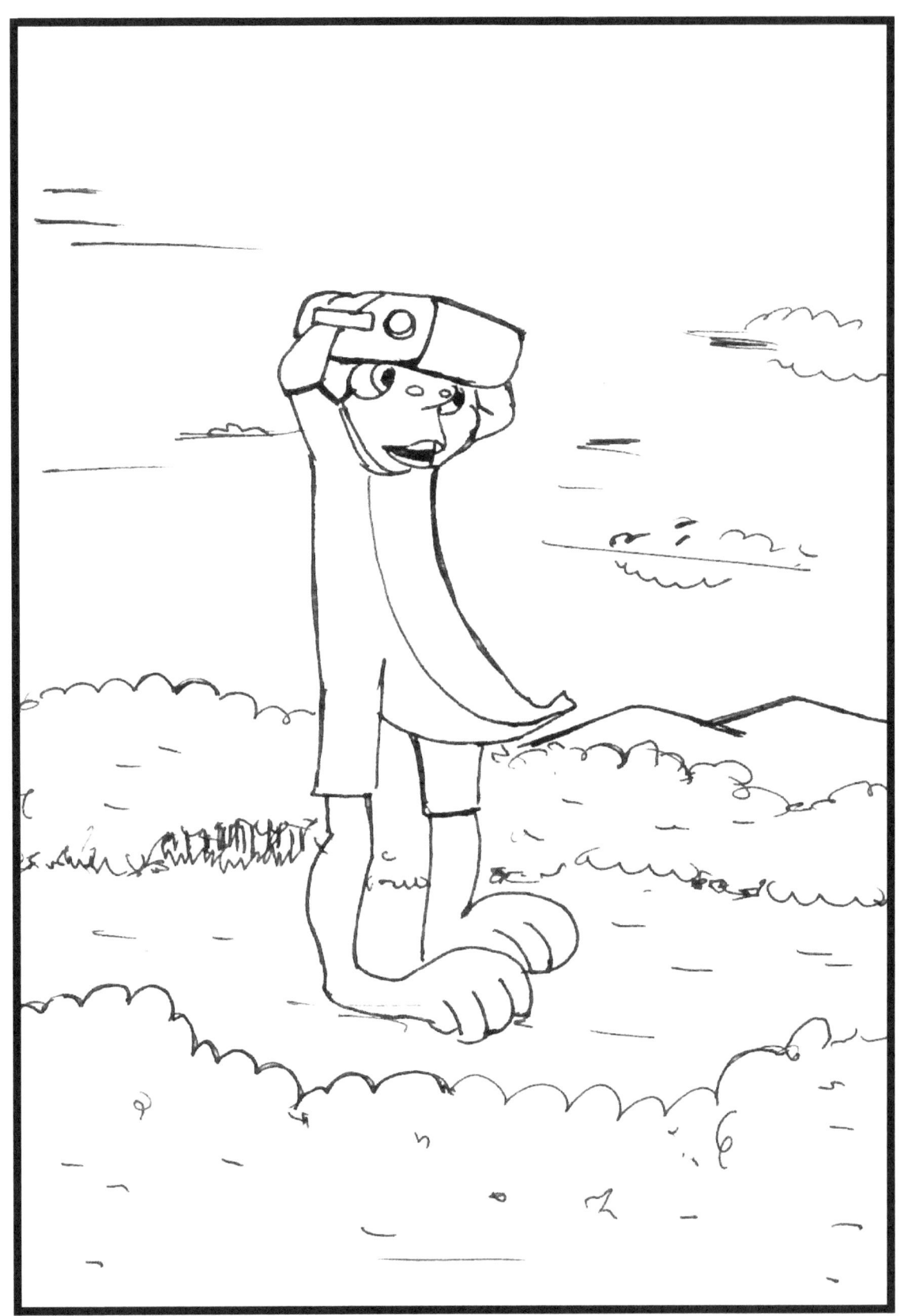

Mr. Banana carrying a jerrycan

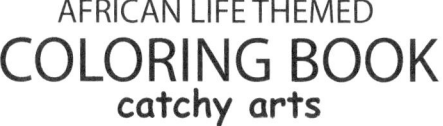

AFRICAN LIFE THEMED
COLORING BOOK
catchy arts

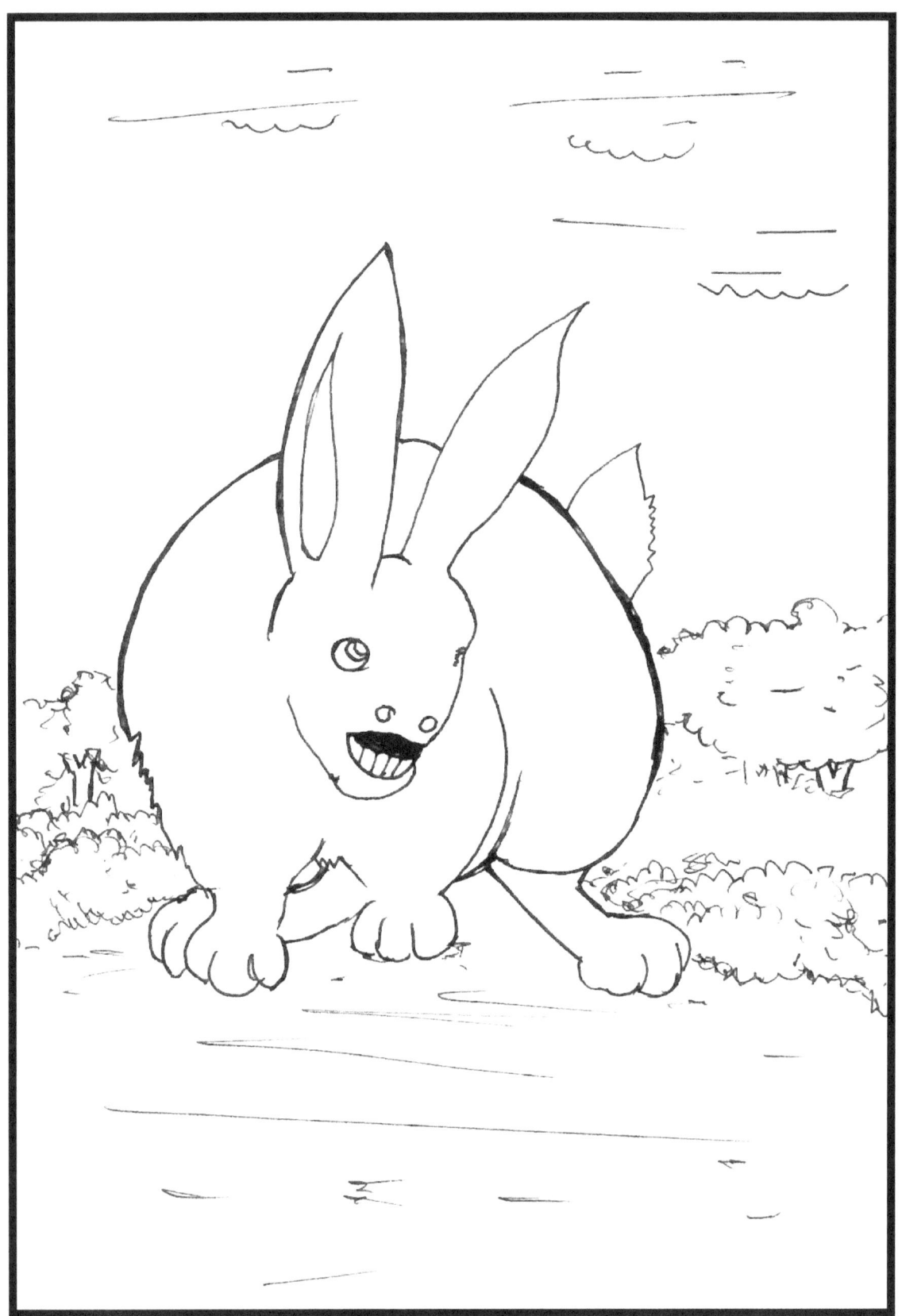

Mr. Rabbit

AFRICAN LIFE THEMED
# COLORING BOOK
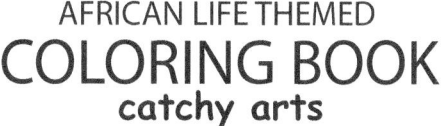
catchy arts

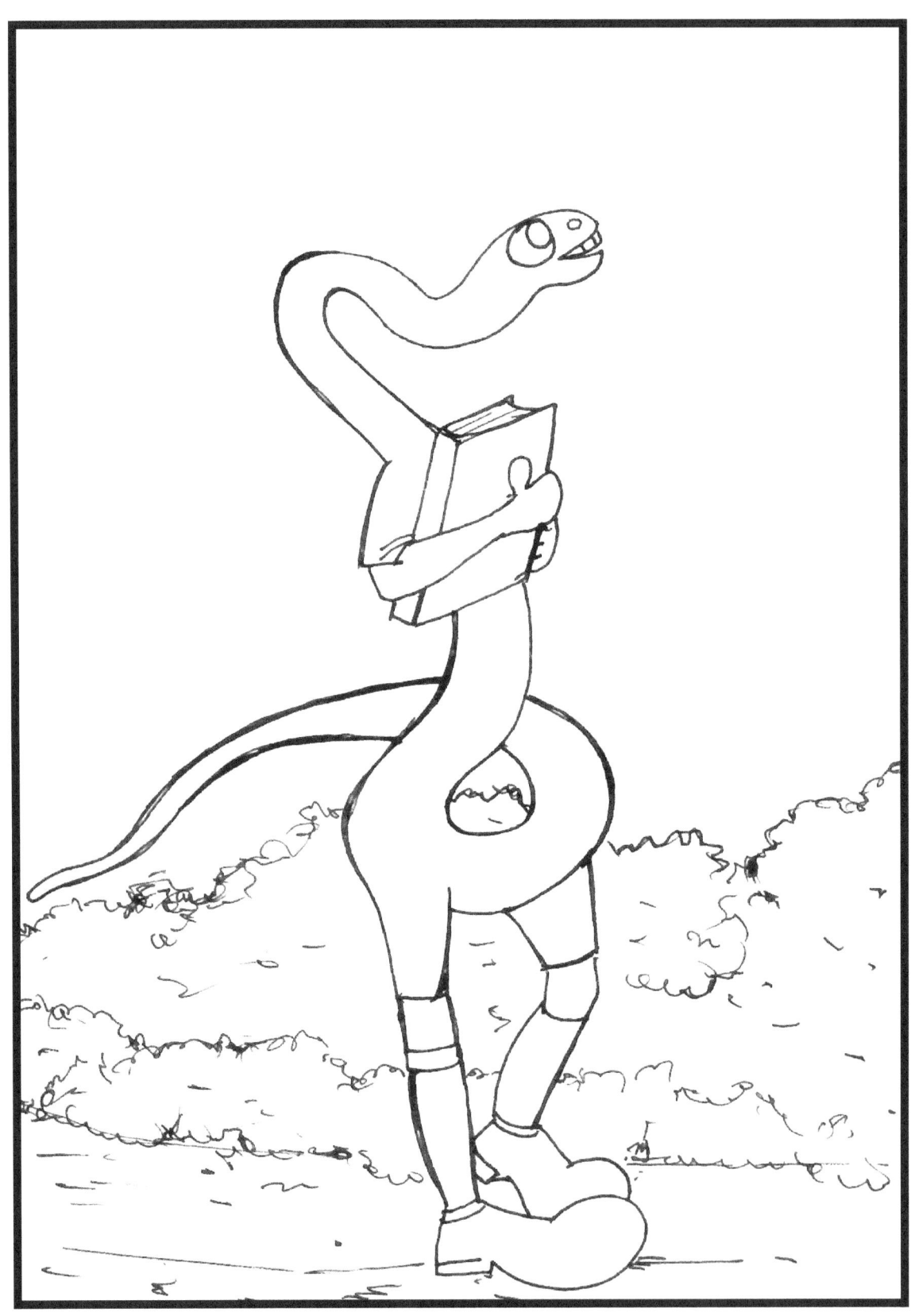

Baby snake going to school

AFRICAN LIFE THEMED
# COLORING BOOK
catchy arts

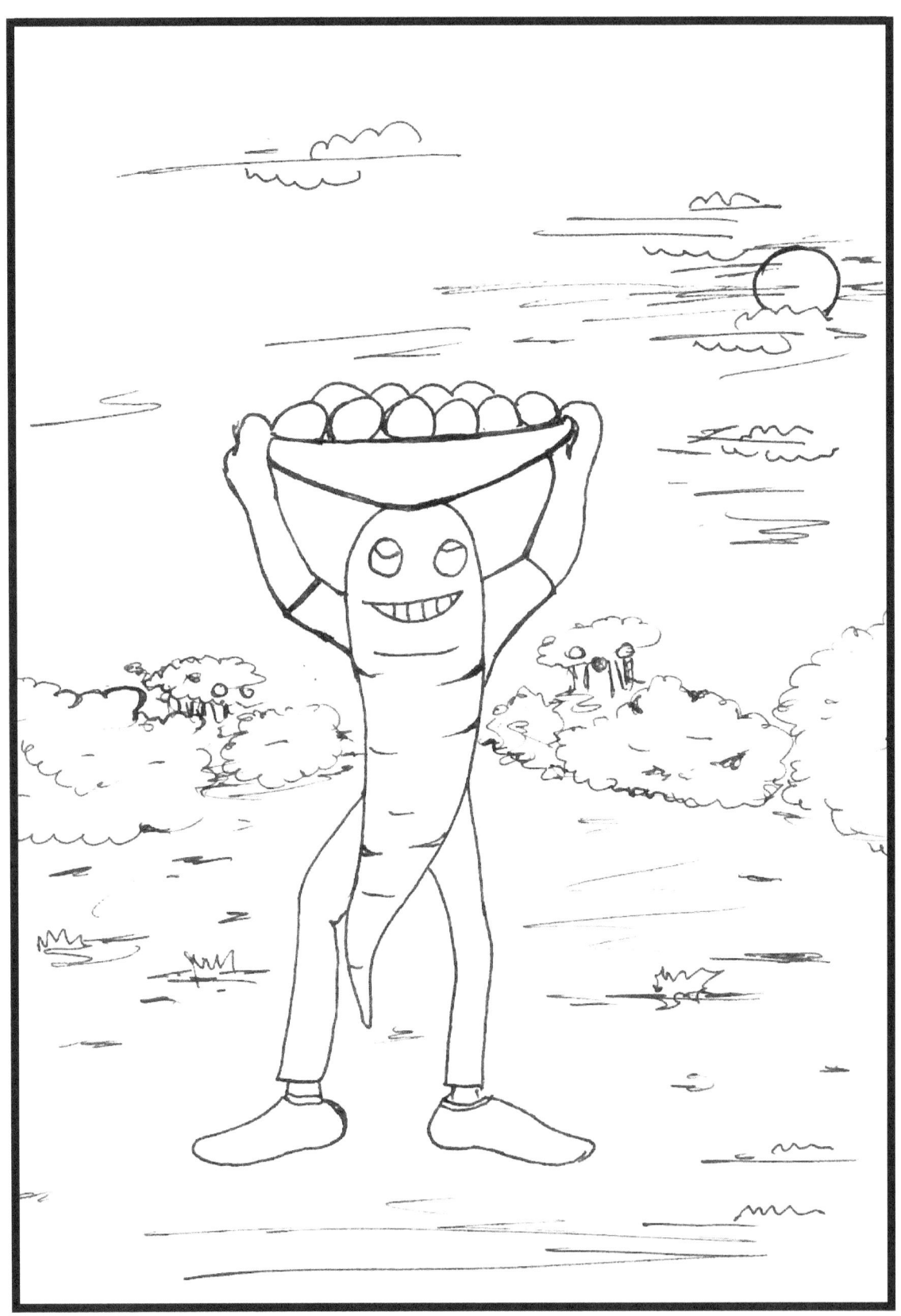

Mr. Carrot carrying the eggs

AFRICAN LIFE THEMED
# COLORING BOOK
catchy arts

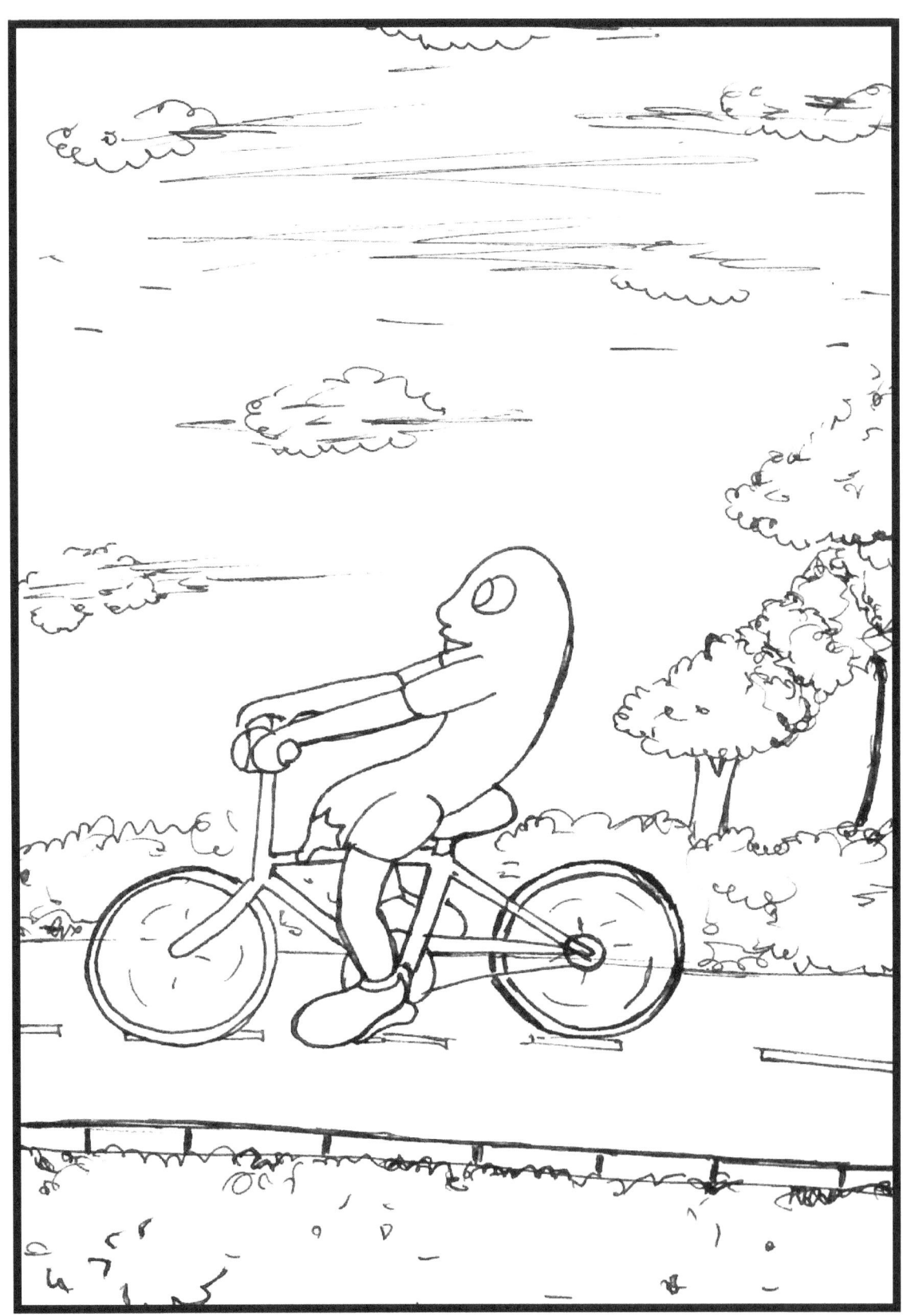

Mr. Eggplant riding a bicycle

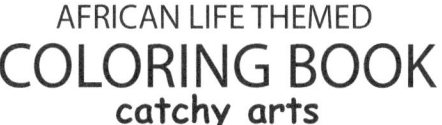

AFRICAN LIFE THEMED
# COLORING BOOK
catchy arts

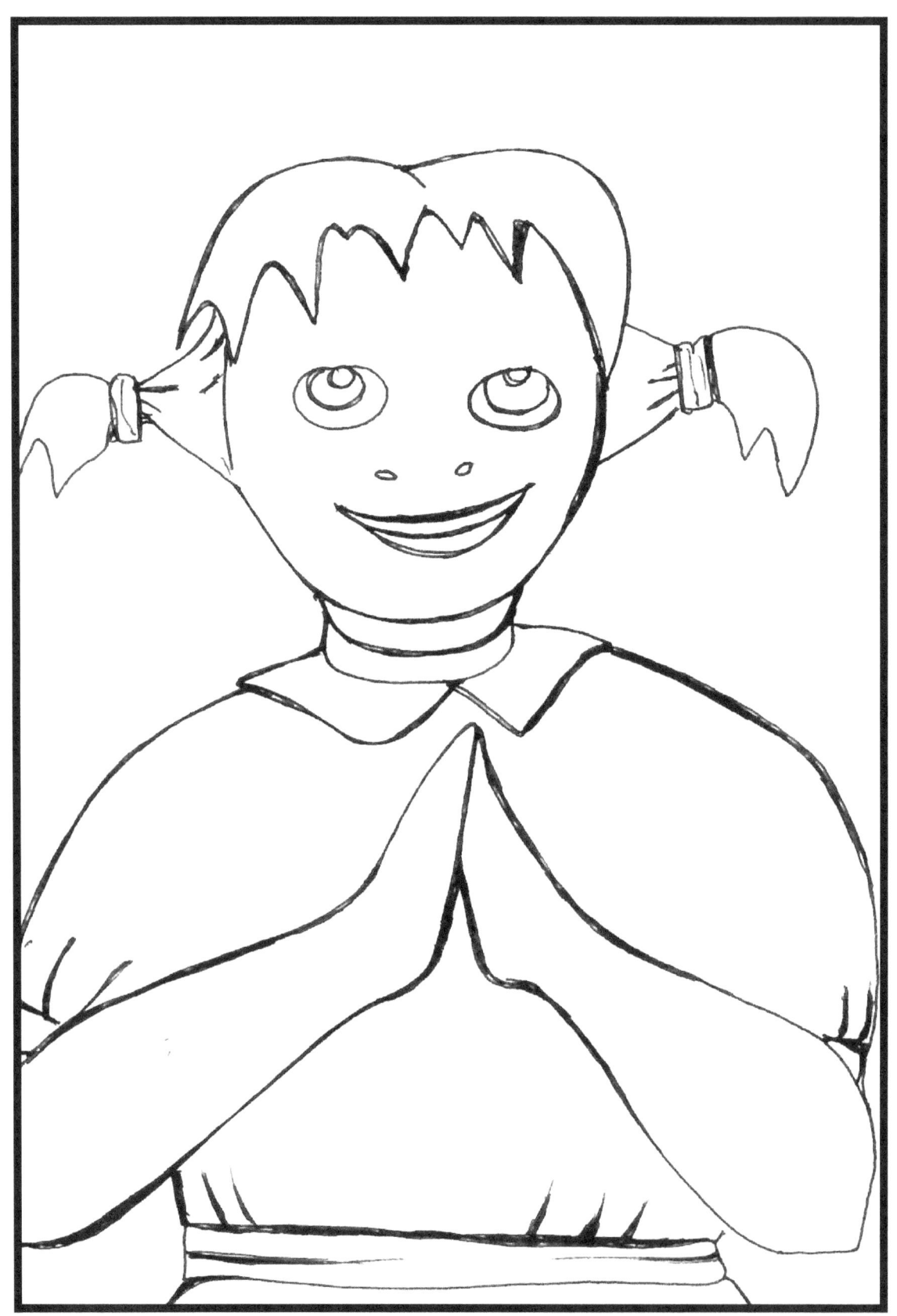

A little girl smiling

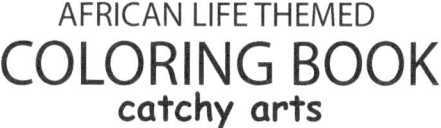

AFRICAN LIFE THEMED
# COLORING BOOK
catchy arts

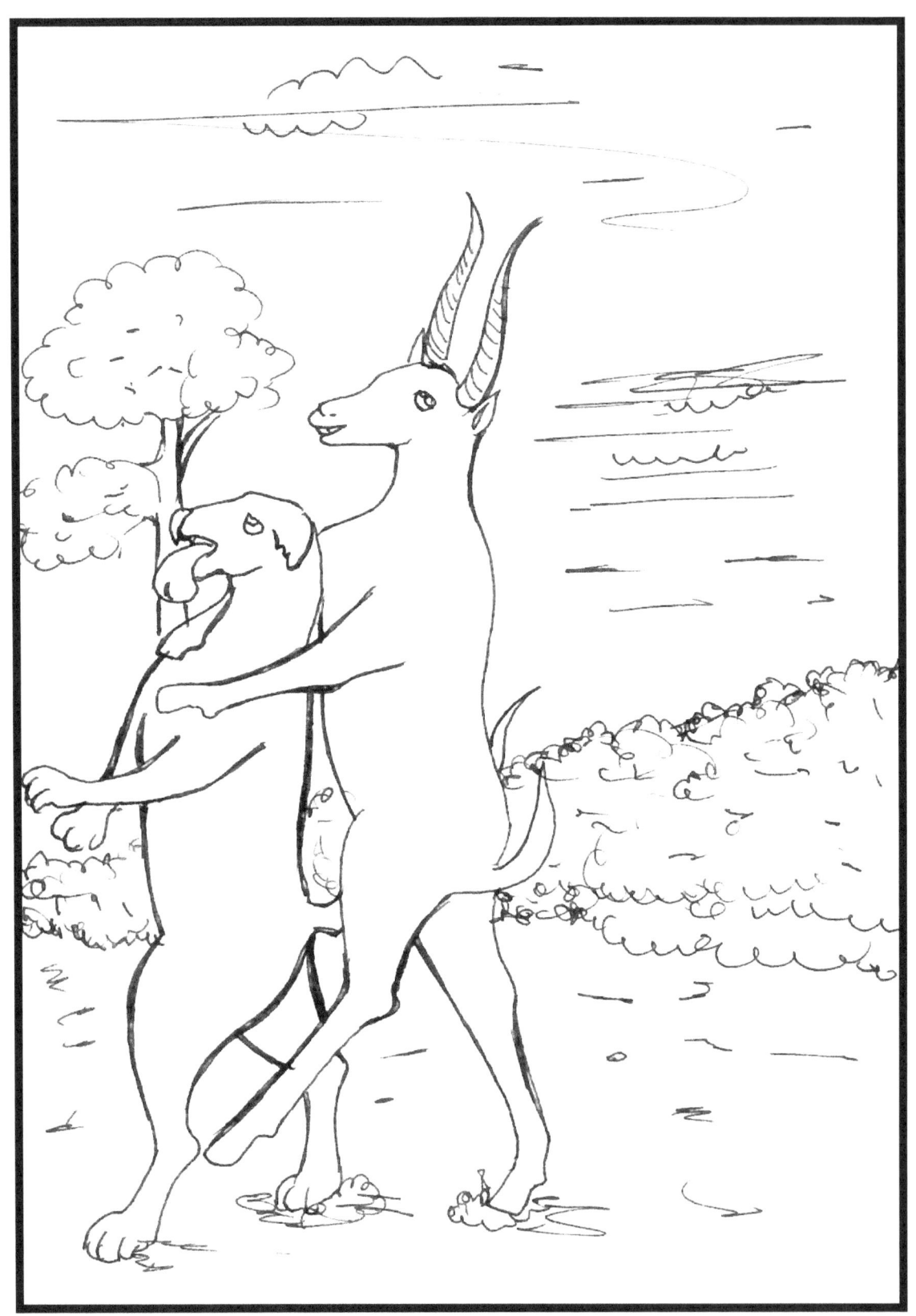

Mr. Hyne and Mr. Goat playing together

AFRICAN LIFE THEMED
# COLORING BOOK
catchy arts

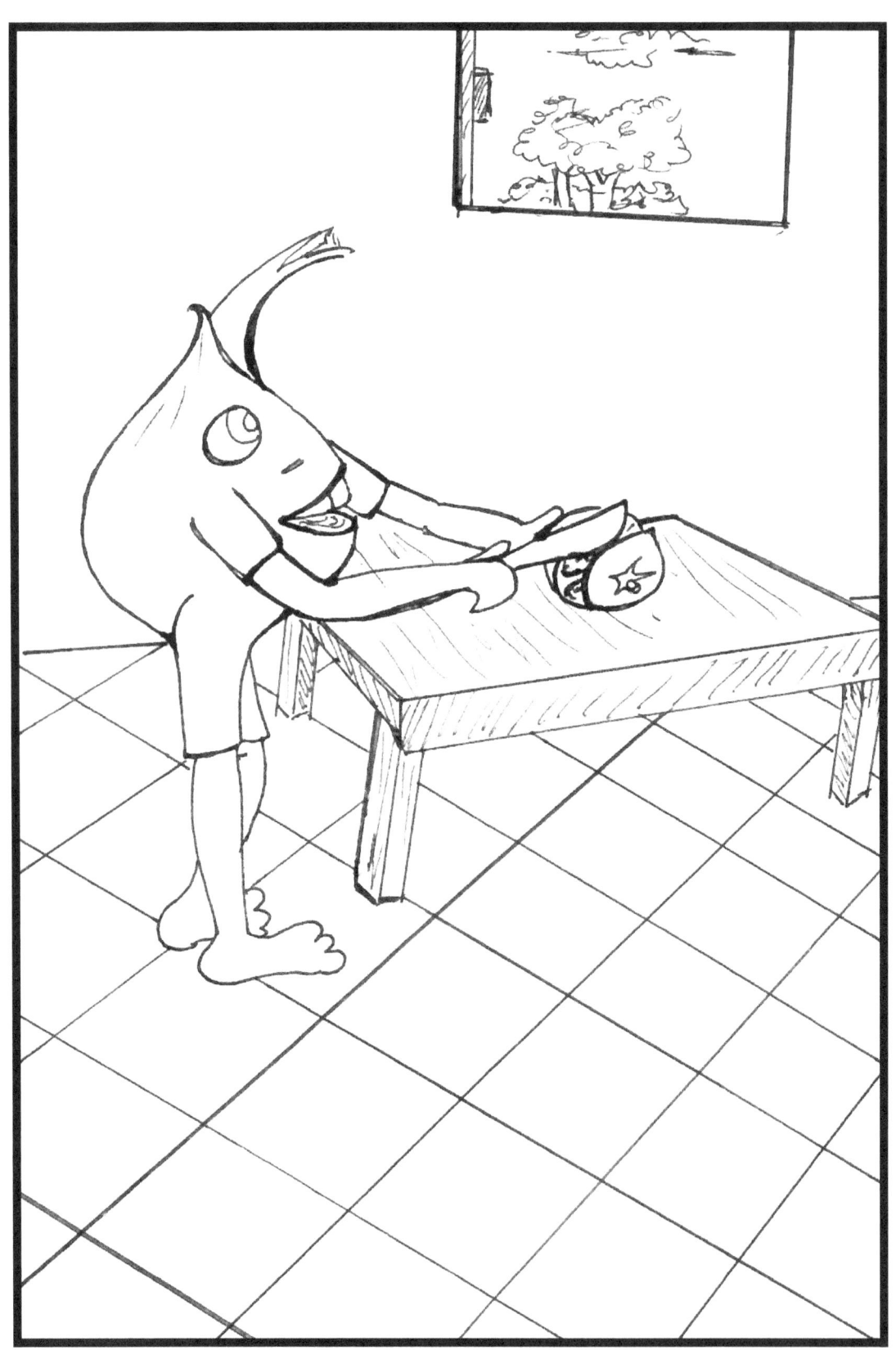

Mr. Onion cutting an orange

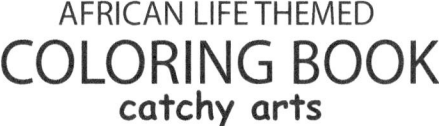

AFRICAN LIFE THEMED
# COLORING BOOK
catchy arts

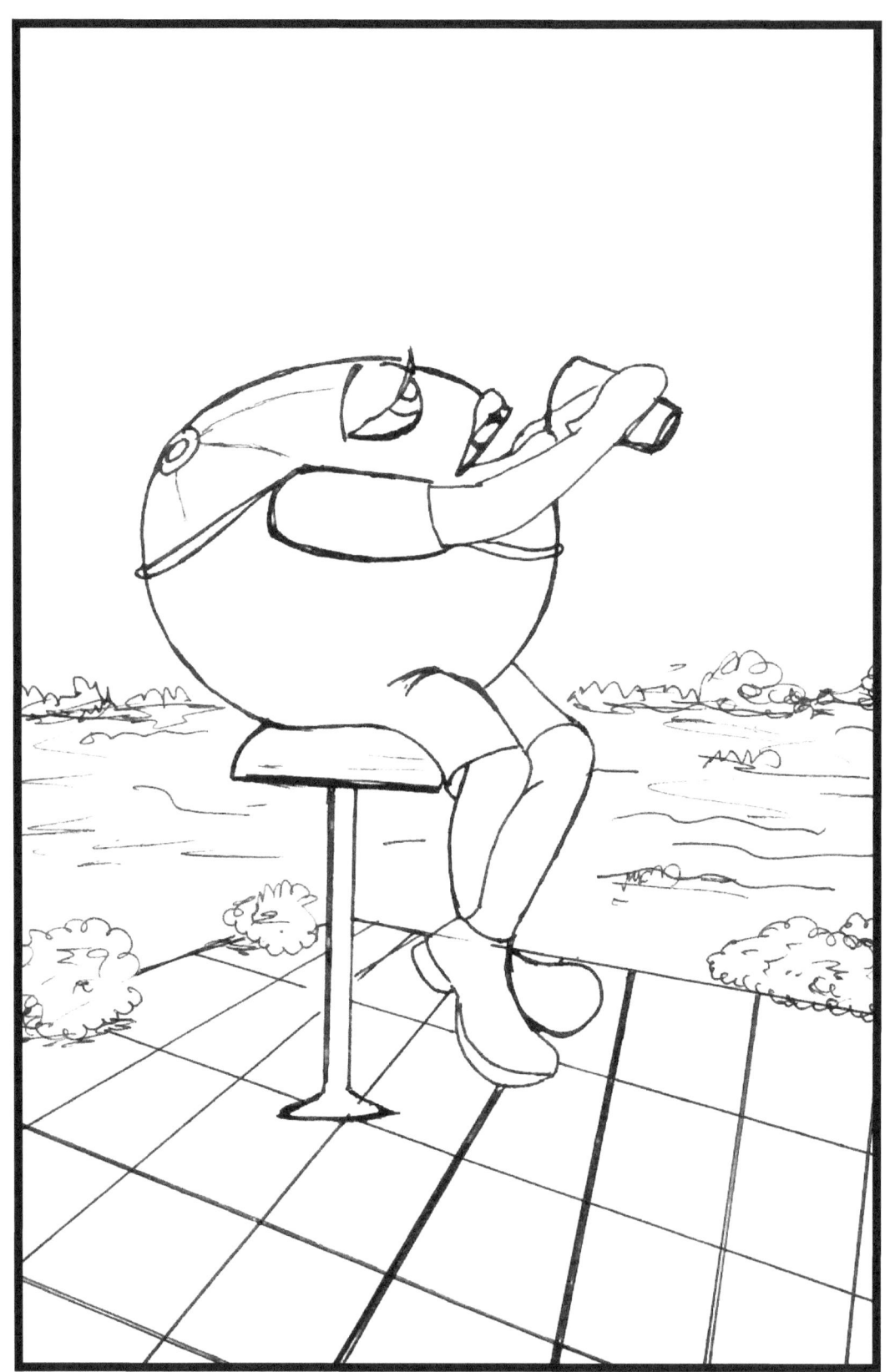

Mr. Orange drinking water

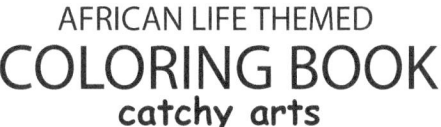

AFRICAN LIFE THEMED
COLORING BOOK
catchy arts

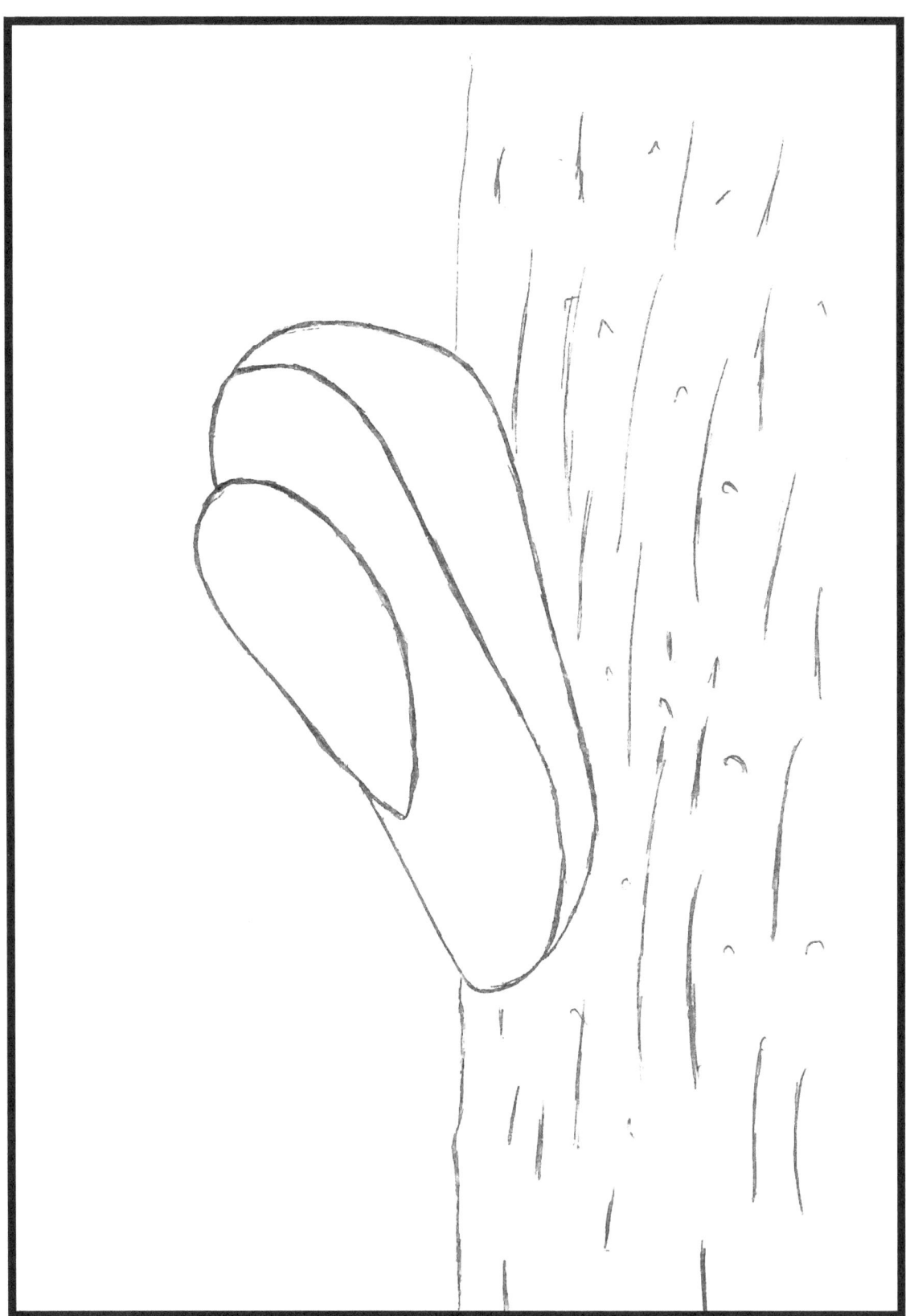

A Beautiful shoe

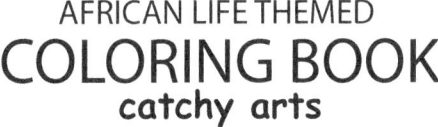

AFRICAN LIFE THEMED
COLORING BOOK
catchy arts

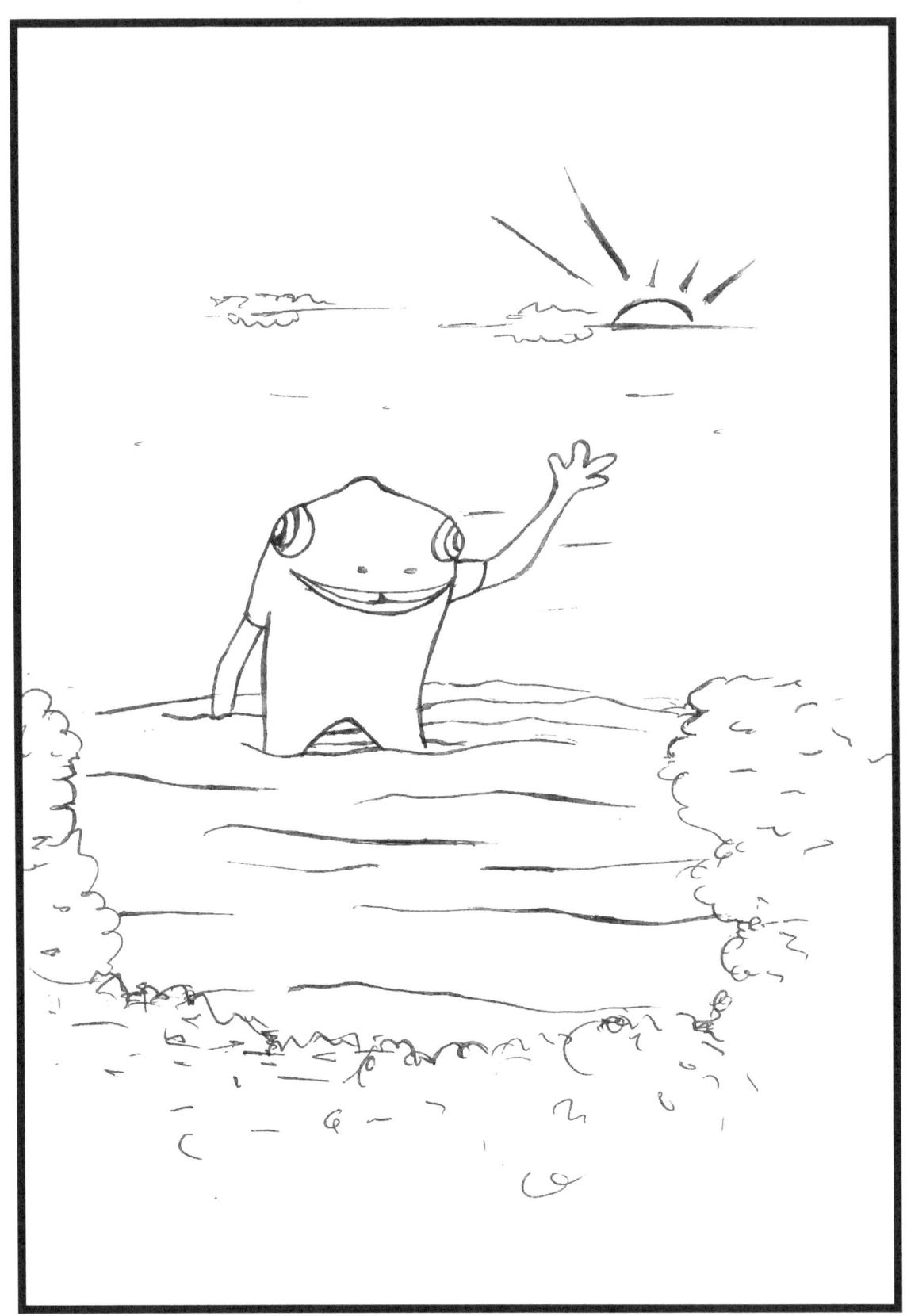

Herman the frog fish waving

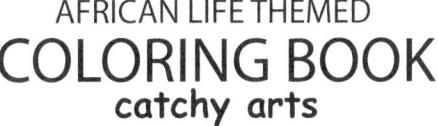

AFRICAN LIFE THEMED
COLORING BOOK
catchy arts

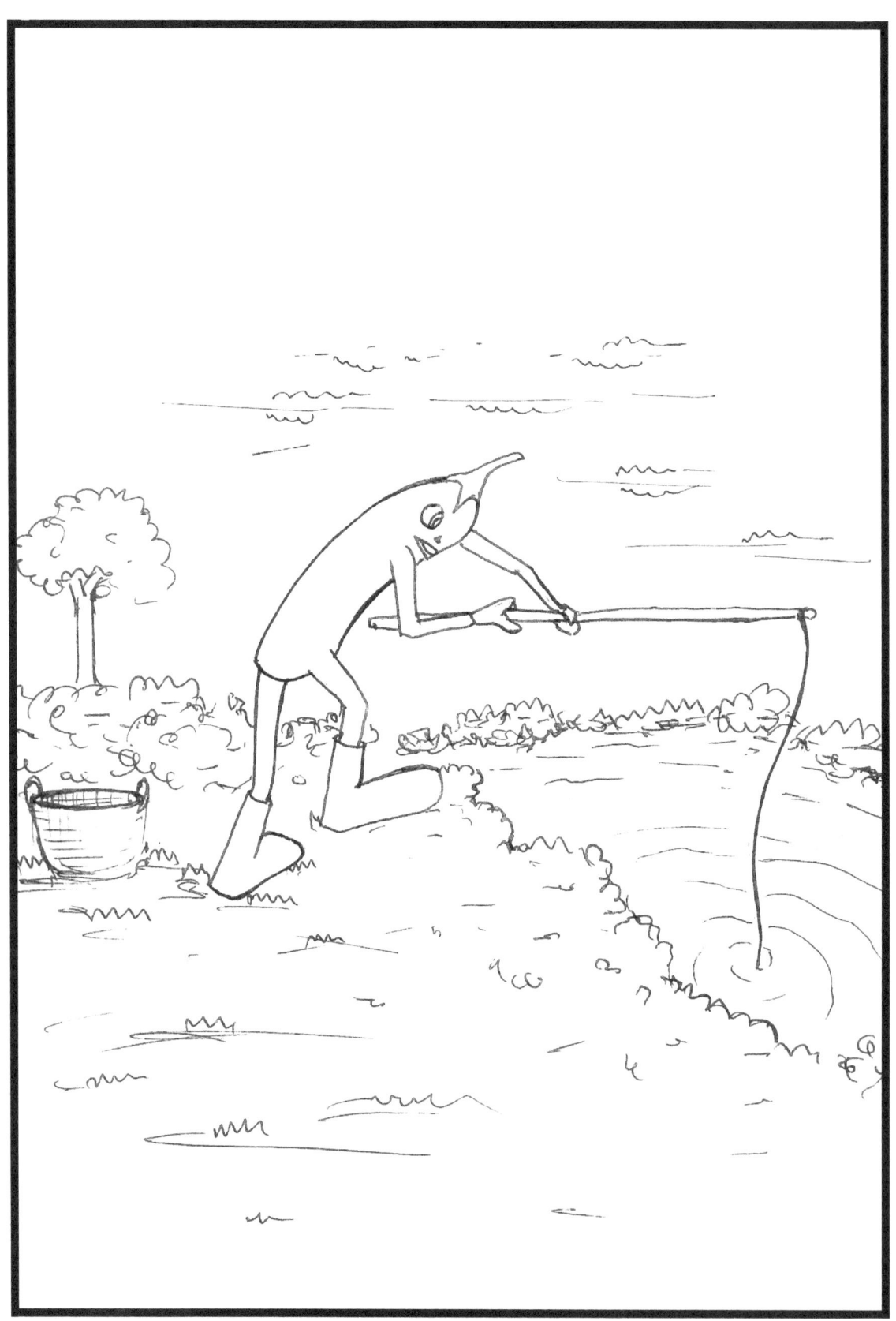

Mr. Eggplant fishing

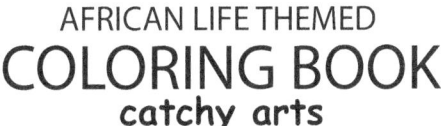

AFRICAN LIFE THEMED
COLORING BOOK
catchy arts

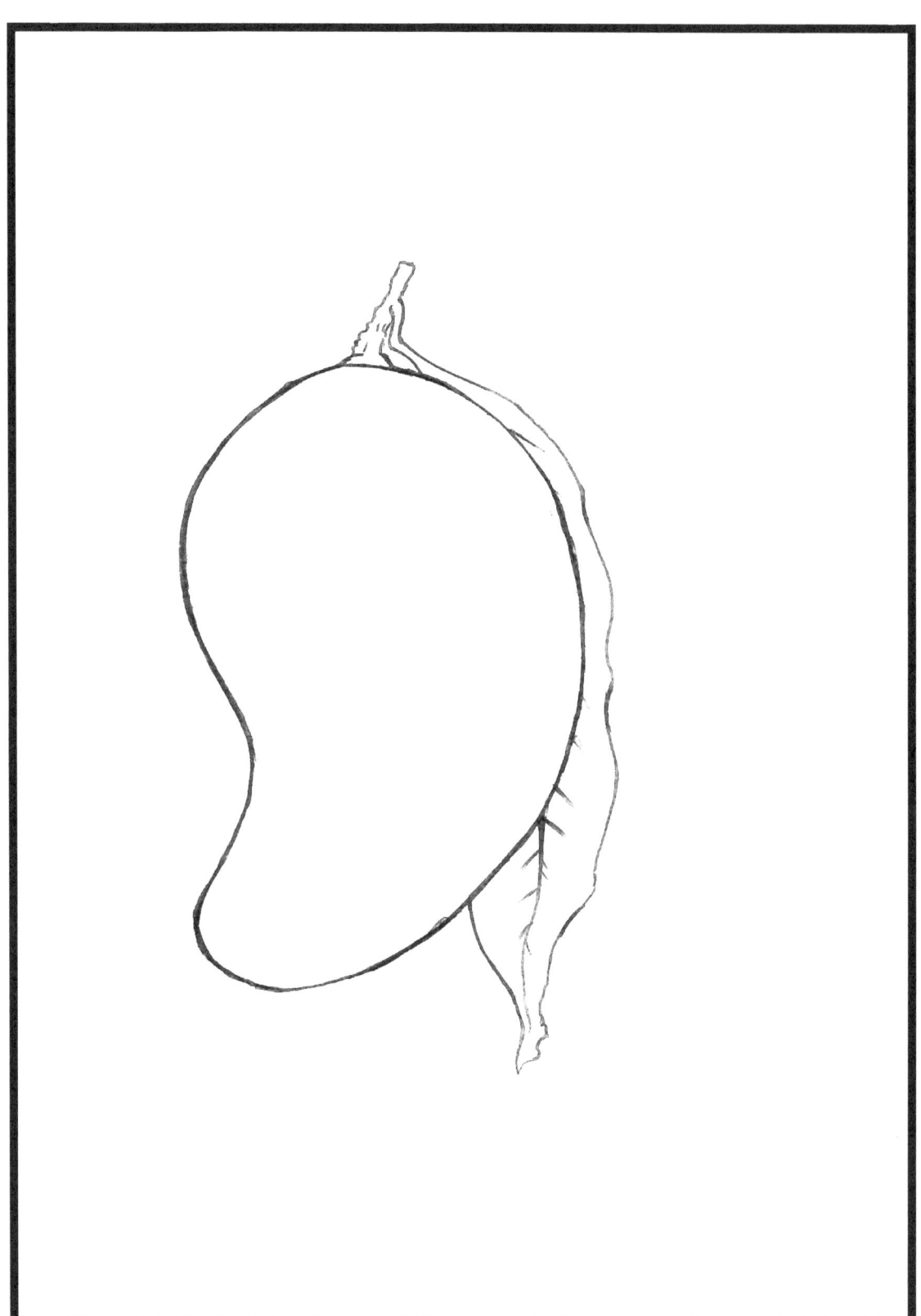

A mango with a leaf

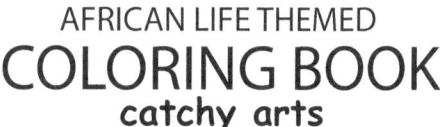

AFRICAN LIFE THEMED
COLORING BOOK
catchy arts

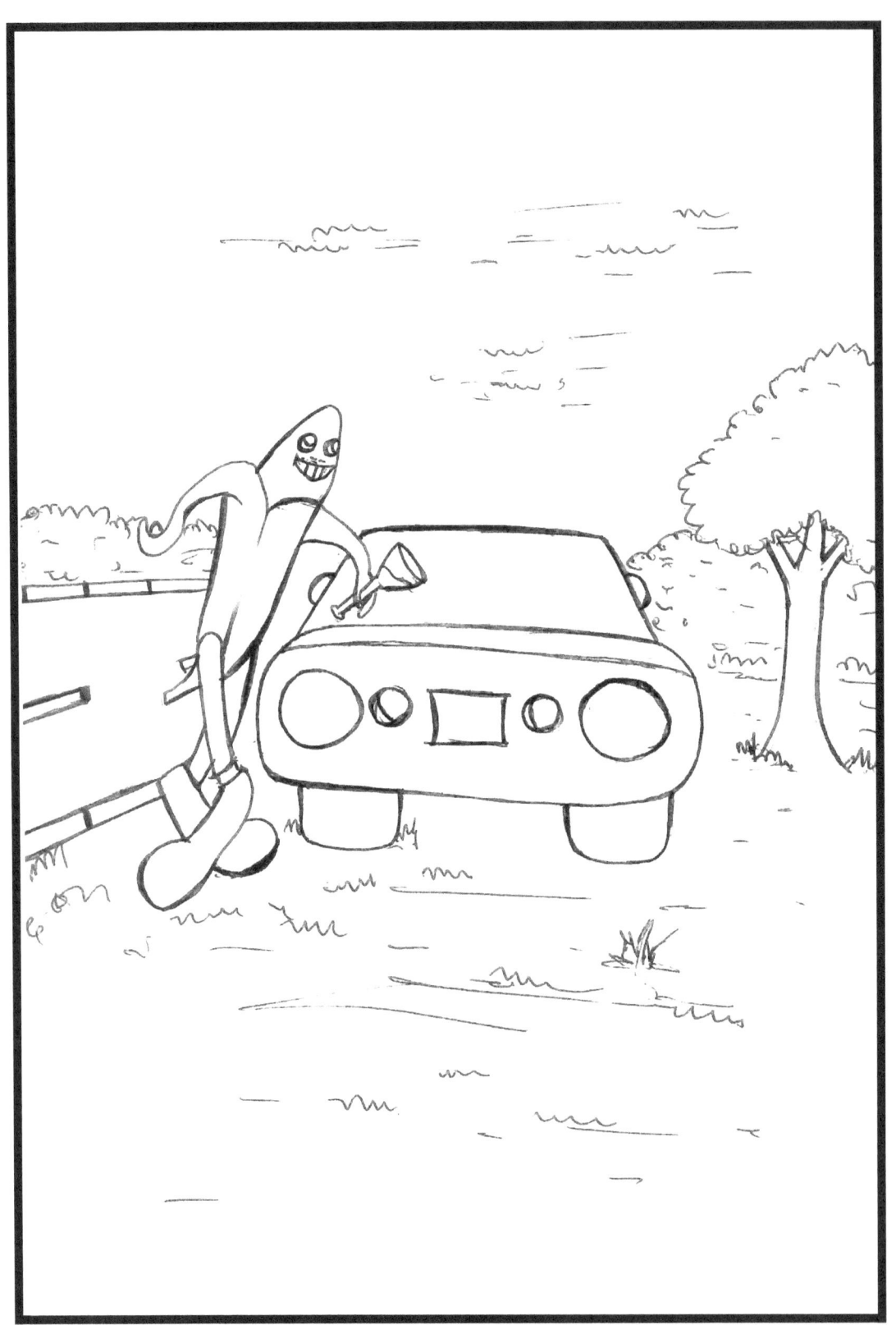

Mr. banana smiling with his car.

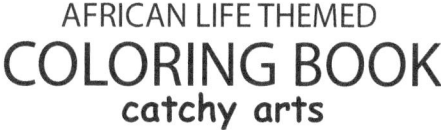

AFRICAN LIFE THEMED
COLORING BOOK
catchy arts

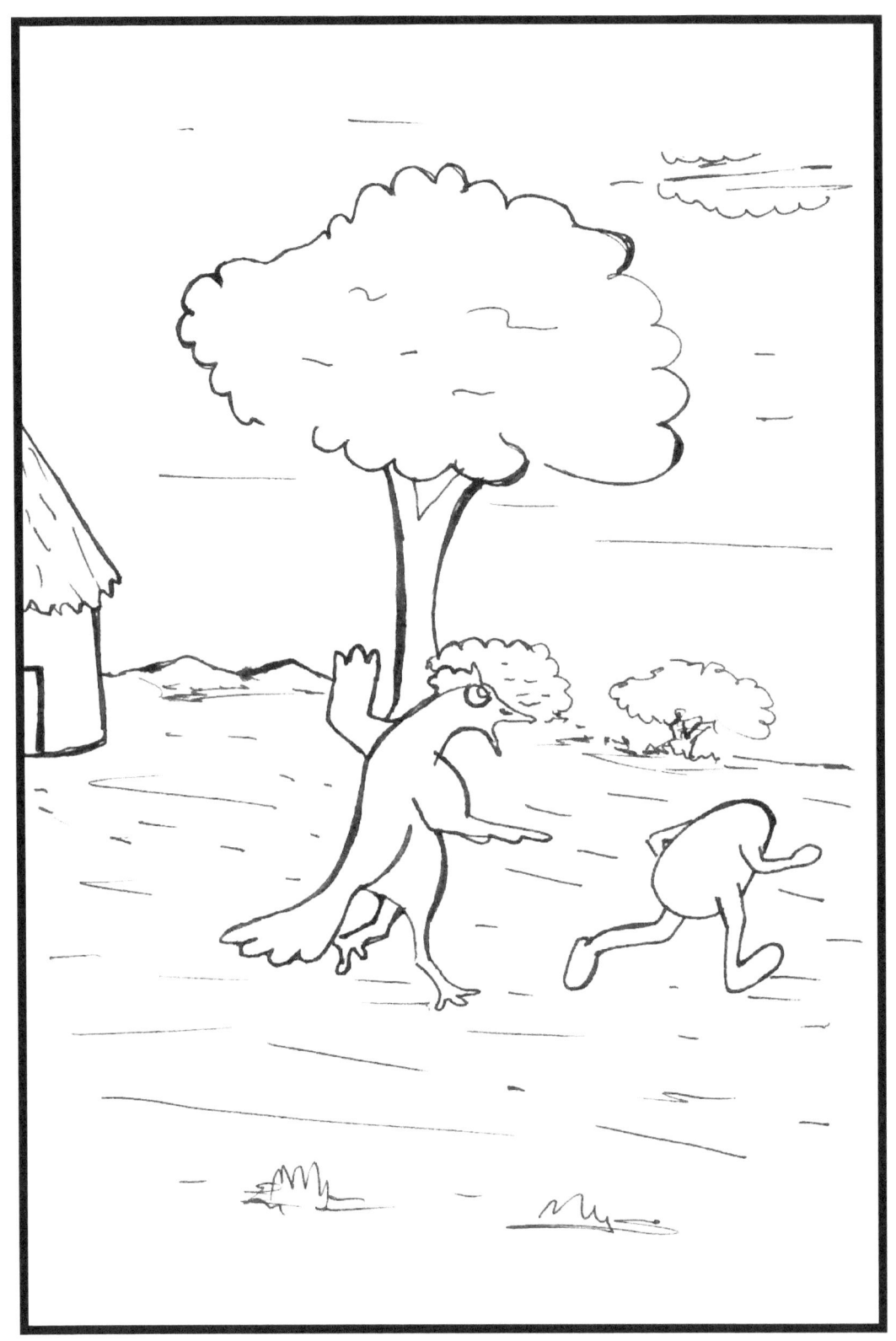

Mother hen playing with a little baby egg.

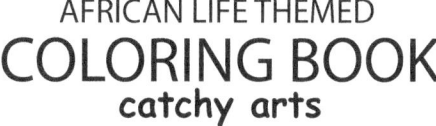

AFRICAN LIFE THEMED
COLORING BOOK
catchy arts

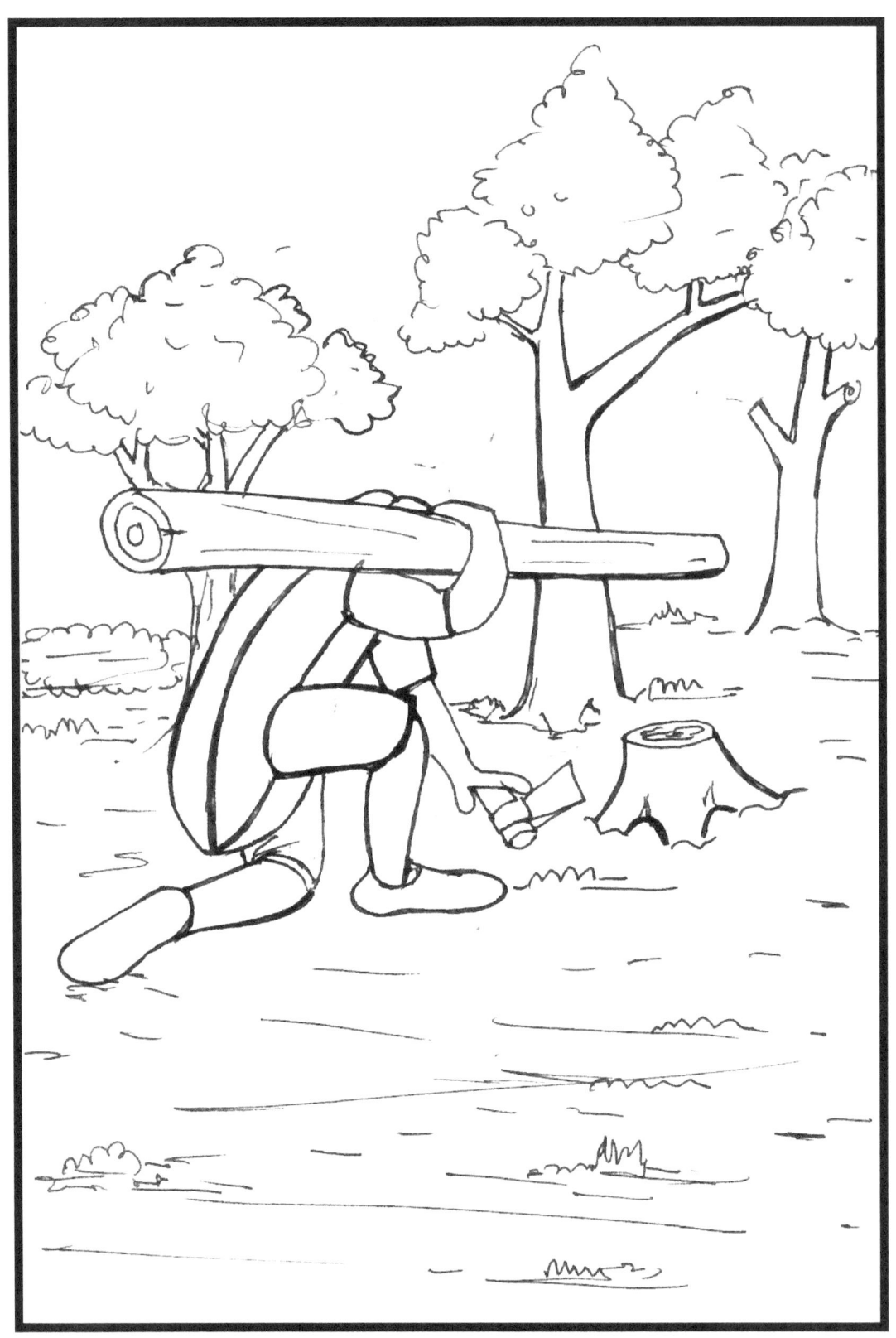

A man carrying wood and picking an axe

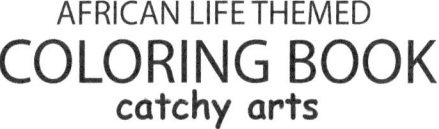

AFRICAN LIFE THEMED
COLORING BOOK
catchy arts

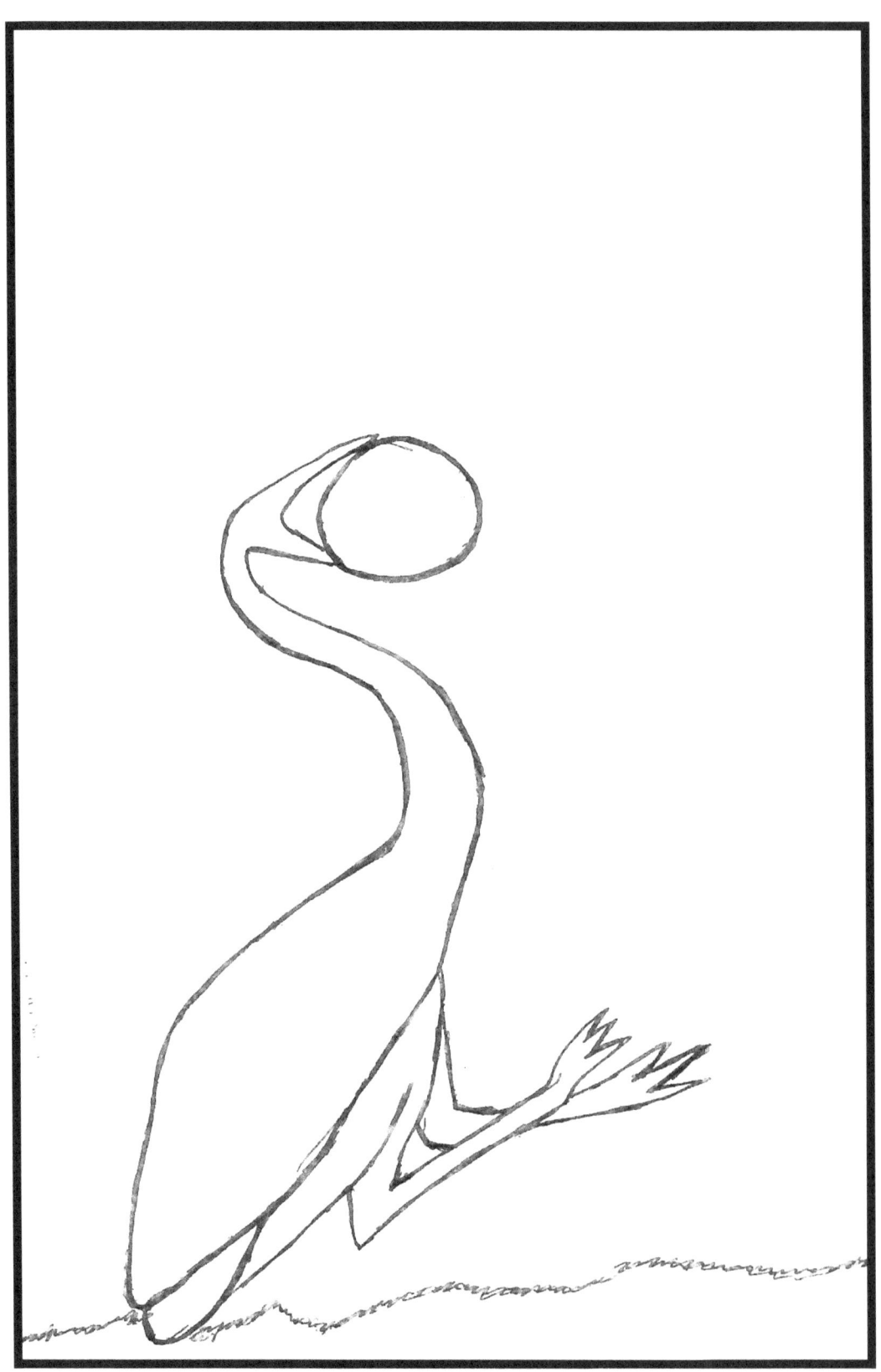

A bird eating a fruit

AFRICAN LIFE THEMED
# COLORING BOOK
catchy arts

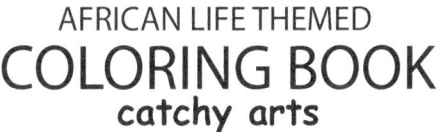

www.ingramcontent.com/pod-product-compliance
Lightning Source LLC
Chambersburg PA
CBHW081008170526
45158CB00010B/2959